248.4

6215

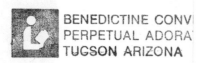

"It is a typical Joan Puls book in the best sense of the word. Throughout the book, she fulfills the expectations raised in her introduction, in particular her thesis that 'if spirituality is more than an abstract ideal, it manifests itself in our human responses to the brokenness of our world.'"

Jan H. Kok
World Council of Churches

"Joan Puls has written her latest book with remarkable authority. Within the milieu of the commonplace she contemplates the deepest and loftiest mysteries of life and death; she addresses herself to the theme of openness as the key to everyday holiness. Again and again she illumines this theme by opening herself to us with sensitivity and quiet humor without self-consciousness.

"The reader is a privileged witness of a moving and intimate faith journey without becoming an embarrassed voyeur of another's inner struggle. The impact is powerful and persuasive. There are no exhortations here. These words ring with the true authority of lived experience."

Frederick R. Wilson
Retired Staff, World Council of Churches

"Joan Puls has again challenged us to lay aside concepts of God and expressions of faith that support theological dualism, urging us to recognize that what is, is God in our midst and that it is in the everyday circumstances of our lives that God chooses to meet us. Her ability to maintain an ecumenical perspective in her reflections on the spirituality of human experience makes this a compelling book for our times."

Frances P. Cunningham, O.S.F.
Past President, School Sisters of St. Francis

Seek Treasures
in <u>SMALL</u> Fields

<u>EVERYDAY</u> HOLINESS

Joan Puls

TWENTY-THIRD PUBLICATIONS
Mystic, Connecticut 06355

Twenty-Third Publications
185 Willow Street
P.O. Box 180
Mystic CT 06355
(203) 536-2611
800-321-0411

ISBN 0-89622-509-7 (Paper)
ISBN 0-89622-555-0 (Cloth)
Library of Congress Catalog Card Number 91-68559

D E D I C A T I O N

to my mother
small field,
with treasures
to the third generation

"The field in which we search is the space and time of your life
and mine. And we are about the rhythm of planting and sowing,
of plowing under and of reaping. The process is sacred. The hope
is always there that with the seed and its silent growing, with the
plowing and its careful upturning, with the reaping and its multiple fruits, the treasure will slowly be revealed....All the days of
our life we plow with the farmer, furrow by furrow, field by
field."

Every Bush Is Burning, pp. 11-12

CONTENTS

Seek
Treasures
in SMALL Fields

Shunka joined our community less than a year ago. She was very small, very dependent, very vulnerable. This rescued puppy has been a parable of openness.

She immediately set about exploring her surroundings, learning her limits, and making friends. Life with Shunka has been an experience of life abundant! She plunges into every available water tank (or fish pond), mud puddle, and river. She is generous with her licks. She plays and tugs and races with every muscle stretched and every sense alert. We attribute our collection of neighborhood friends, young and old alike, to Shunka's exuberance and warmth.

Jill, our next-door neighbor, also has a dog, as well as a husband, a grown son, and a ninety-year-old mother. In addition, she opens her house to half a dozen small children whom she minds while parents work. Her door open, her attention full, she is counselor and comforter to many in the area. And she has a part-time cleaning job. She doesn't talk about church and she doesn't use religious language. She is the Good Samaritan of Wolseley Road.

Everyone in Britain sat motionless in front of their TV screens and waited for one man to alight from the RAF aircraft in Wiltshire, England. We needed to see with our own eyes and hear for ourselves what inner strengths had sustained this man during five years of captivity in the Mideast. When John McCarthy walked free, we all experienced a new degree of freedom. This human being, an ordinary television journalist, had clung to hope against the odds of defeat, despair, and insanity. Where had he wandered, what had he learned, what was his secret? Who is this man now?

When my partner, Gwen Cashmore, and I began leading ecumenical retreats in various parts of the British Isles, we presumptuously titled our exploration of new ways of being church "One, Holy, Catholic, and Apostolic." Understandably, we ran into dead-ends: murky theological concepts, deference to present or absent clergy, stagnant notions of institution and structure. We concluded early on that a more human language was needed and a focus on human life with its range of joys and tragedies. As Karl Barth put it, "What is Christian is secretly but fundamentally identical with what is universally human. Nothing in true human nature can ever be alien or irrelevant to the Christian....Much in true human nature is unrelated to religion, but nothing in true human nature is unrelated to the Christian faith."[1] Or, in Dietrich Bonhoeffer's words: "In what way are we the 'ekklesia,' 'those who are called forth,' not conceiving of ourselves religiously as specially favored, but as wholly belonging to the world? Then Christ is no longer an object of religion, but something quite different, in deed and in truth the Lord of the world. The church stands not where human powers give out...but in the center of the village."[2]

If church-belonging and the ecumenical movement have a basis in reality, it is because they are rooted and experienced in the very places where we live and work, in the communities that encircle us, in our unexpected and routine encounters. If spirituality is more than an abstract ideal, it manifests itself in our human responses to the brokenness of our world, the threats to our planet home, the crisis points in our own lives, and the pleas and plight of human beings around us. Ecumenism and spirituality meet their challenge in the midst of the long-lasting troubles in Northern Ireland, in the dilemmas of relating to Iraq and its minority populations, in the failure of economic systems to distribute food and medicine to those most in need, in local situations of pain and tension and controversy. This is not to deny the value of private and communal prayer, theological dialogue between churches, reading the mystics, or practicing "spiritual exercises." It is to put them in perspective.

As a Franciscan engaged as a consultant in spirituality, and as someone who lived the monastic way, at least for a part of my religious journey, I have always felt closer to the experience of lay seekers than to any specifically religious or clerical club.

Only recently is a spirituality for lay Christians being distinctly articulated. I would like to think that this volume is a small contribution to the search and the exposition. It is the claim of these pages that any place, any time, any circumstance of life, is an invitation to enlarge and deepen our spirits. In *Every Bush Is Burning* I underscored the miracle and the mystery of the everyday. In *A Spirituality of Compassion* I traced the patterns of exchange in familiar encounters and experiences. *Hearts Set on the Pilgrimage* asked questions about our corporate claims to be church and probed our faithfulness to the gospel. This book is about openness, that attitude and condition that is at the heart of all spirituality and all ecumenism.

The first chapter attempts to locate "spirit" and "spirituality" in human as well as gospel terms. Each of the next ten chapters looks at one of the "givens" in our life: time and place, work and community, limitations, loneliness and doubts, freedom and food, and the stranger. They are some of the stuff of which life, everyday life, hence spirituality, is made. Each of them is a call to openness, to vulnerability. Once we push back the boundaries that delimit and define us, once we pull apart the threads of meaning within the "given," we open ourselves to the breadth and depth of human experience. It seems to me this is what Jesus was about in the gospels, pushing back the limits imposed from without or within, expanding the borders of human life, enlarging ordinary experiences, and introducing new and deeper questions and challenges. The final chapter summarizes the basic questions and the basic conditions for discipleship. Who qualifies for entrance into God's commonwealth, the community of gospel-followers?

I could be criticized for selecting a wide variety of common experiences and then skimming over them in a haphazard and ambiguous manner. I accept that criticism. But I also feel it is valid to point in certain directions, to raise questions, to start a dialogue, and, above all, to suggest areas for reflection that others can probe and pursue with their own expertise and against the background of their own life evidence.

"The Holy Spirit is that power which opens eyes that are closed, hearts that are unaware and minds that shrink from too much reality....Vision and vulnerability go together."[3] Let those who have ears to hear, eyes to see, hearts for breaking, continue!

I WILL PLACE A NEW SPIRIT WITHIN YOU

"I shall give you a new heart and put a new spirit within you. I shall remove the heart of stone from your bodies and give you a heart of flesh" (Ezekiel 36:26).

If there is one phenomenon that characterizes contemporary religious search, it is the quest for an authentic spirituality. Feminist, monastic, ecumenical, creation-centered, spirituality of struggle: Each has its proponents and advocates. Each has its literature and its pursuits. Charges of pantheism, escapism, activism, elitism shadow some of these quests. Whether the focus is a renewed discipleship, a healing of dualisms, or a search for personal meaning, the issue is "spirituality."

It is unfortunate that this abstraction, spirituality, has become the common parlance. The potential for misinterpretation is obvious. For some it signals a split between the physical or the natural and that which is spiritual. For others it connotes an interior movement away from life's realities and human tragedies. For still others it is a private journey of prayer and conversion. Its ambiguity has led today's disciples to turn it into "holistic spirituality."

The Scriptures are more concrete and perhaps more accurate. "I will place a new spirit within you" (Ezekiel 36:26). "Renew a right spirit within me" (Psalm 51). "My spirit rejoices in God my Savior" (Luke 1:47). "Into your hands I commend my spirit"

(Luke 23:46). "If you do not have the spirit of Christ, you do not belong to Christ" (Romans 8:9).

There is nothing abstract or vague about Ezekiel's "stony hearts." We all know the reality: hardheartedness, indifference, an incapacity to feel, to respond, to love. I am inhabited, says Jesus in Luke 4:18, by a spirit, pervaded by it, so that the entirety of my life is evidence of this occupying spirit. To be possessed by a spirit is to be consumed, taken over. The spirit of our lives is our total self, who we really are. It is the self that is not confined to time and place. It is the self that spans all our experiences and responses. It is the self that is our truest being. Spirituality is the process that leads to true selfhood. If we are Christians, it is a movement into Christ's spirit.

"Spirit" becomes tangible and concrete. Some years ago I went with friends to visit Gethsemane Monastery in the hills of Kentucky. As we stepped out of our car a jolly-looking monk, driving a small truck, asked us, "What brings you here?" "Thomas Merton," we answered. "His spirit lives on," he called back. And in those quiet woods and simple chapel, it was not difficult to feel the current that Merton had sparked in the hearts of all who are searching, connected to each other and to divine purposes.

I have often attempted to describe the spirit that animates St. Ben's in Milwaukee. It permeates the nightly meal, which provides regular nourishment to numerous homeless and poor, and the Sunday service, which attracts a wide variety of seeking and serious-minded Christians. The spirit is best summed up as "hospitality," in Henri Nouwen's words: "Not a subtle initiation to adopt the lifestyle of the host, but the gift of a chance for the guest to find his or her own."[1] Such is the message of the welcome and openness in that inner city refuge.

Occasionally when I am with ecumenical groups over a period of time, I recognize a familiar spirit, quite unlike that of other conferences or gatherings. It is a mingling of quiet respect and a family atmosphere. I experience a sense of belonging together, coupled with an appreciation for the complexities and struggles that have brought us together.

Over the years I have come to understand this "new spirit" of which Ezekiel speaks, and the spirit that possesses Jesus, in a distinctly new light. It is in opposition to what is worldly in Paul's terms (though it is not dualistic): "Do not be conformed to the world where you live, but rather be transformed through the renewal of your mind" (Romans 12:2). Ezekiel's "new spirit" does have an interior dimension, though it is not separated from life and reality and the human condition. Rather, it probes them, holds them in a contemplative gaze, and proffers healing and hope. It is personal and involves prayer and conversion, but it is not private.

On the contrary, the final word about the life of the spirit, or spirituality, is that it is a movement *into relationship*, a journey entirely dependent on those who influence us, those who journey with us. The "new spirit" we seek is permanently stamped by the spirit of others, past, present, and to come. The "new spirit" is one that has been embraced by Christ, in his fullness (the cosmic Christ), and one that embraces the family and the world Christ entrusts to us.

IDENTITY AND RELATIONSHIP

Nothing is more mysterious or fascinating than the identity of a human person. What lengths we go to in our craze for psychic understanding to uncover the mystery of personhood! We search for clues in enneagrams and aptitude tests, we hope for insights from therapists and spiritual directors, we pursue psychoanalysis, we look to genetics and heredity, to the movement of the stars and planets. The question Who Am I? haunts us, occupies, lures us.

> "Who am I?" They often tell me
> I stepped from my cell's confinement
> Calmly, cheerfully, firmly
> Like a squire from his country house...
> Am I only what I myself know of myself?
> Restless, and longing and sick, like a bird in a cage,
> ...Weary and empty at praying, at thinking, at making.
> Who am I? This or the other?
> Who am I? They mock me, these lonely questions of mine...[2]

Discovering one's identity is a favorite preoccupation of human beings. Looking into our psychological mirrors is just one degree more engrossing than our fascination with the identity of others. Lovers never tire of the question: Who is this person, my beloved? Even parents ask in bewildered tones: Who are these individuals, my children, bone of my bone, and yet so unfathomable? No matter how carefully we study each other, there is no perfect frame or definition. Something always escapes us, an elusive transcendent quality. "If we live our own humanity with authenticity, we are confronted with that mystery at every moment...the mystery of the human being."[3]

Are not all of these questions an effort to name the spirit that dwells within and animates us? The Hebrews called it "ruach," wind, or breath. "Ruach is a different kind of power associated not so much with being alive as with being a person. We might call it the power of personhood, the power of separate otherness, the power by which we are recognized as ourselves. But it is also the power to recognize, and to be impinged upon, by the otherness of persons, things, realities which are not ourselves."[4] Our spirit resides only in our potential or actual relatedness to some other.

If we read the gospels carefully, we notice how Jesus' identity was an obsession for those around him. Who is this man? Where did he get all this knowledge? By what authority does he command the wind and the seas? We know where he is from, but we are in the dark about his real origins, the real source of his power, his real identity. Jesus himself had a certain penchant for questions of identity. Who are my mother and brothers? Who is my neighbor, who is greatest, who is servant? Who do you say that I am?

Jesus' questioners were motivated by curiosity, to be sure, but also by anxiety. Who are you? meant: What relationship do you have to us? What does your presence demand by way of response, or reaction, from us? And he names those roles and titles—mother, neighbor, servant. They are determined not by blood or arbitrary definition, but by a quality of relationship. Identity only becomes real if there is authentic relationship issuing from the spirit. We are who we are because of those to whom we relate, and we act and become according to their impact and influence.

As Christians we believe that Christ's spirit became available to us through Jesus' resurrection. Our relationship to Christ profoundly alters our identity. We are reborn, consecrated, anointed, sent. Isabel Carter Heyward says: "Imagine the resurrection as a seed planted in the soil of Jesus' decomposition and harvested forever in his friends' subsequent refusals to give up the intimacy and immediacy of God...What began between Jesus and those who love, and were loved by him, continues among these lovers of humanity."[5] There are echoes in the words of Oscar Romero: "If they kill me, I will rise again in the Salvadoran people." It is one continuous spirit. Jesus' investment in life, in relationship, bears fruit in the lives and relationships of all who follow him. Identity is immortal. His spirit lives on, the monk said of Thomas Merton, in you and in me. The spirit of Francis of Assisi, and Mike and Nettie Cullen—the inspirations for the nightly meal at St. Ben's—live on in the Milwaukee banquet. The spirit of Pentecost lives on in the *oikoumene* and its many manifestations today.

Explicitly as Christians, and implicitly as human beings, we seek to know by what spirit we are enlivened. One fruitful approach is to discover to whom we belong. Who are our people? With whom are we connected by common breath? It is a question I ask myself frequently in this "in-between" existence of mine. My family, my religious community, many of my friends, are elsewhere. My mission at this time is in the United Kingdom. "My people" are constantly in flux. I have made new friends here, as I did another time in India and Switzerland. The people I meet at retreats and gatherings and with whom I explore faith and discipleship are my people. Difficult as it is, I live "in the gaps," in the opportunities to relate briefly, intensely, continuously, across divides of time and space, through written messages and brief encounters, through shared commitments and dreams. "My people" expand and contract, move forward into focus and back again into silence. It is a rhythm, a dance. My world is a human circle. "My spirit is engrafted with the spirits of those who journey with me."[6] As I develop and sustain contacts with the world church, I like to think that my people include communities of reconciliation in Ireland, prisoners of conscience to whom I have written, circles of women as far distant as North India, base communities in São Paulo, ecumenical communities in Taizé or Iona, justice and peace groups in Germany.

"Do not ask me to abandon or forsake you." Ruth's words to Naomi have taken flesh in every age and under very diverse conditions. Missionaries, all who have been sincere companions of the searching and struggling at whatever level, have experienced the displacement that incarnation requires. Those who offer shelter to the homeless and to abused women and children, L'Arche workers and AIDS helpers, Sanctuary workers and Witnesses for Peace, communities like Corrymeela, know the meaning of "Your people shall be my people; wherever you go, I will go."

Tell me who your friends are and I will tell you what you stand for. Our spirits are etched by those among whom we live and work. We become like those to whom we give ourselves. The gospels remind us again and again of that truth: "Whoever makes herself lowly, becoming like this child, is of greatest importance in the reign of God." "Which of these was neighbor to the one who fell in among robbers?" "The blind see, the deaf hear, the lame walk...blest is the one who is not scandalized by 'my people.'" "The Human One came to give his own life as a ransom for the many."

We are led to the people with whom we are to form community. J.V. Taylor speaks of "annunciations," those experiences in which we become mutually aware of the common path we are to tread.[7] Jean Donovan wrote of her reasons to stay in El Salvador: "Several times I have decided to leave. I almost could except for the children, the poor, bruised victims of adult lunacy...Whose heart would be so hard as to favor the reasonable thing in a sea of their tears and helplessness? Not mine, dear friend, not mine."[8] The movement into Christ and Christ's spirit is made in company with others and on behalf of others. "Spirituality is a community enterprise. It is the passage of a people through the solitude and dangers of the desert, as it carves out its own way in the following of Jesus Christ."[9]

Our identities are intertwined. We are the carvers and creators of one another's spirits. Without relationship, we quickly sink into non-being. The Holocaust, says Isabel Carter Heyward, became a mirror in which we saw our capacity to reduce one another to ashes.[10] We have the power to extinguish human identity, as we have the power to bring human life to wholeness and ecstasy.

FREEDOM AND UNPREDICTABILITY

Origins, background, and education are no guarantees of the direction any person will take. The most unlikely among us become leaders and saints and rogues. We do not know our own hidden desires. What we are to become has yet to be revealed. Daniel Ellsberg rose from the ranks of U.S. journalists to become a voice of conscience about Vietnam. Who would have selected Beyers-Naudé as the ordinand to become the voice of anti-apartheid in the Dutch Reformed Church? I remember a young friend of mine some years ago telling me quite emphatically that justice was not her thing. She now ministers among the poor immigrants of southwest Texas.

Just as the Spirit breaks into our daily lives, so do we "break through" the patterns and images by which others know us and by which we even view ourselves. "The Spirit blows where it will," Jesus said to Nicodemus, and so it is with those begotten of the Spirit. They are free, unmanageable, uncontainable. It is the reason for not passing judgment, for giving people the space to create and to risk. When the element of surprise departs from our spirits, we are pronounced dead.

There was a moment in Jesus' life when the Spirit broke through in a vivid and dramatic manner. "Suddenly the sky opened and he saw the Spirit of God descend like a dove and hover over him. With that, a voice from the heavens said, 'This is my beloved son. My favor rests on him'" (Matthew 3:16-17). It was a moment of election, of affirmation, of anointing. We know that at other times the desired accolades were not forthcoming. When he faced antagonistic questions from the Pharisees no voice spoke out on his behalf. In the garden of Gethsemane, there was only silence and the steady breathing of the friends who slept. On the cross, Jesus heard the taunts of the soldiers, but they were not overruled by any heavenly interference.

There was that moment in the synagogue when Jesus boldly proclaimed the words of Isaiah and their fulfillment in his own person. He was possessed with a confident, prophetic spirit. We can almost feel the tension as his words broke through the reserve and suspicion of those who listened. Jesus continued to surprise and to disarm his followers and his enemies. He spoke as one having authority. His answers to legal questions were unconventional. His very attitude to the law was unpredictable. He associated with those at the fringes, he avoided the plaudits of the crowds, he turned the standards that governed daily life upside down. Jesus was a paradox even to his closest friends.

For us, too, there are those rare experiences of anointing and assurance. I felt certain on my first trip to India that I was sent in the name of my entire religious community. It was a powerful source of confidence and strength. During a retreat with fellow ministers of hospitality at the St. Ben's community, another person and I were called forth and asked to anoint each member of the group gathered. It was as close to an ordination as I hope to come!

But I remember, too, the more common experiences of lonely discernment, of risky decision making, when I longed to know whether I was moving in the right direction, where I might find human support, whether I could trust my own instincts. I heard no sounds of encouragement. I felt the weight of the world on my shoulders. But breakthroughs have come in those moments, too. Once I made the decision, or definitely stepped over the fence, I felt the strength of my own conviction and the energy that comes with ownership of a particular truth.

Jesus was jolted on occasion. He met his match in the Syro-Phoenician woman who pointed out his insularity and parochialism. "Even the dogs under the table [the Greeks] eat the [Jewish] family's leavings" (Mark 7:28). There was the centurion who trusted Jesus' power: "Just give an order and my boy will get better" (Matthew 8:8). Mary Magdalene ignored social custom and human respect. We must believe that they all influenced Jesus' thinking and attitudes.

Lucky are we if we are nudged into new interior places by the bold freedom and spontaneous deeds of those around us. I am inspired by a man who has taken illegal occupancy of a deserted house to call attention to the plight of the homeless. I have been embarrassed into action on behalf of justice by the gentle chiding and willing risks of a friend. I am in admiration of a young father of a family who works closely with political prisoners in Belfast. We have the potential for rebirth and transformation, as long as we remain vulnerable to new experiences, to all that we have not yet learned. As long as we can see the extraordinary shining through the ordinary, and are capable of awe and delight and raw emotion. As long as the faithful pursuit of a mystery is more important than certitude and approval. As long as we trust our intuitions and our dreams. As long as we recognize truth even in surprising places: the lips of a child, the lyrics of a song, the words of a condemned criminal.

Our freedom, with its corresponding ambiguities, is both a gift and a responsibility. Out of every concrete situation comes the challenge to respond, spontaneously and authentically. "A human being must be able to determine what form the expression of his virtue should take in the light of the particular situation in which he finds himself; he must be able to influence every situation, and he must be able to participate in determining all of them."[11]

Moses was afraid of the burden of leading others into the unknown. "I cannot carry all these people by myself, for they are too heavy for me" (Numbers 11:14). God's response was to gather seventy from among the people. "I will take some of the spirit that is on you and bestow it on them, that they may share the burden of my people with you." And when Moses was apprised of those who were prophesying without credentials, he exclaimed: "Would that all the people of the Lord were prophets!" Is not that the strength of belonging to a Christian community, where we are all called into the freedom of God's spirit, where together we discern and decide and dare? Our freedom is inextricably linked to the lives of those around us, even those far distant from us. We are bound to wear it with some trepidation.

THE POWER OF TRANSCENDENCE

Human beings, threatened, crushed, battered on all sides, transcend the pain and the horror and begin again. We have that awesome power. The scenes of the Armenian earthquake were almost more than we could bear to watch. And yet we know that men and women and children rose up from the debris of their lives and started anew. The Lockerbie plane crash haunted all of us, with its sudden tragic interruption of so many human lives. A fourteen-year-old boy became the symbol of grief and loss. His parents' bodies were never found. He buried his ten-year-old sister. His home was destroyed in the crater. And yet he lives. We meet it again and again, in situations of war, of exile, of illness and death, of physical disabilities. Persons whom we think will break under the weight of grief astound us with their capacity to rebuild, to embody the courage of the human spirit and its power to rise up from ashes; to break through pressing burdens and heavy mists and stand again in an open space, stripped of everything, still transcendent. "I said to my soul, be still, and let the dark come upon you...I said to my soul, be still, and wait without hope."[12]

H.A. Williams's *True Resurrection* pursues this theme in depth. When someone who knows herself only as clod and clumsiness in the water actually becomes a swimmer, she experiences transcendence. So with the tennis player and painter who have mastered their crafts, the lover who is released into new wholeness.[13] When I look at one of my books, the product of hand and mind and heart, I understand a mite more about transcendence of spirit. When human beings become more than we or they ever thought they could be, we glimpse transcendence, the power of love to light up a shadowed face, the power of acceptance to beautify a deformed body, the power of forgiveness to ease a troubled heart.

In the presidential election of 1988, Lee Atwater's name became synonymous with ruthless politics. To win the presidential campaign he manipulated the worst fears and prejudices of America's voters. He was successful. Then he was struck down with an inoperable brain tumor. In his dying days, at age 40, Lee Atwater experienced a kind of resurrection. He spoke openly of the wealth and power that he had achieved that was now empty and un-fulfilling. He saw that what was missing in society was what he, too, had lacked, a spirit of kindness. It was not too late, at least for him personally, to face and own that truth.

Membership in one body heightens and strengthens this pow-er. How would we endure tedious tasks and daily dis-couragements without the accompaniment and encouragement of our friends and co-workers? I heard a delightful story from Poly-nesia. It is the custom, so the story goes, for those being ferried to repeatedly call out to the captain, "Thanks!" And the ferryman calls back, "Thanks for your encouragement." So the chant con-tinues, each encouraging each, until the journey is complete.[14]

Together our actions, our visions, our efforts, transcend the sum of our individual contributions. There is a power for renewal in the Roman Catholic church that is directly related to its uni-versal membership and its opportunities for solidarity. We do not always recognize it, but it is partially because of Latin American liberation theology, because of the convictions of many U.S. wom-en, because Indian Catholics are inserted amid other world re-ligions, that there is an impetus and momentum for change and renewal. It was the openness of the community Jesus gathered that gave it a quality of radical universality.

We often say that the privilege of the ecumenical movement is its opportunity for exchange. Our pooled treasures, our combined wealth of tradition, ritual, and faith experience enrich us all and enable us to rise above the limitations and parameters of our sin-gular experience. Locally and regionally, we reinforce one an-other's questions, erase suspicion by our friendships, overcome history by our acts of repentance. An assembly gathers members of the world church, and the most unlikely dialogue and crossing of boundaries takes place.

Life within another culture soon opens up this mysterious transforming power. Having experienced a bit of Indian culture, of European lifestyle, I am now more than an American. My spirit has tasted food that makes my former diet inadequate. I live in a larger world, benefitting from the diversity and the multiplicity of its resources. In an image I've grown fond of, we move from our particular denominational and cultural puddles into life's expansive ocean. As Christians, we symbolize and ritualize this absorption into one another's lives and destinies whenever we gather around the eucharistic table. It may be an occasion when simple food is simply shared or one where Christians are fortifying themselves for pending dangers and death. In that community event, we transcend the particulars of time and place, we share a feast that is (or should be) available to all, and that transforms and empowers us. As Christ is available to us as nourishment and companion, so we become food and sustenance for one another.

This membership one of another also has its devastating effects. Our power to destroy also transcends our individual capacities. No human being alone could threaten a nuclear war, no single part of our globe could manipulate a greenhouse effect. Tyrants spawn injustice, and oppressive systems are born. Drug dealers conspire, and a subculture emerges. Economic and social pressures combine and impinge on one another, and the result is a violent society.

Jesus said: "The spirit of the Lord is upon me...He has sent me to bring glad tidings to the poor, to proclaim liberty to captives, recovery of sight to the blind" (Luke 4:18-19). The spirit with which Jesus was anointed was a spirit of re-creation. Jesus was not sent to bless and to make promises to the poor, to assure them that a reward awaited them for their faith and their patience. Jesus was sent to transform their present situation, to bring justice where injustice dwelt, to bring freedom to those in bondage and sight to those in darkness. In the same spirit, we take up as much as possible the mission of renewing our earth and one another, of dismantling the missiles, of preserving the rain forests, of redeeming our lifestyles, our choices, our relationships.

For many of us the call is to restore vision to our churches, to our religious enclaves. Changing perceptions is a particularly difficult task. "If you were blind, there would be no sin in that. But we see, you say, and your sin remains" (John 9:41). Our vision is narrow and limited and we are prone to deny whatever does not correspond to pre-fashioned images. Sometimes we see anew only after we have been ejected from our established places, stripped of our biased spectacles. Letting go of our faded and prejudiced theories, our blurred vision, will be gradual and painful. "You keep saying: I am so rich and secure that I want for nothing. Little do you realize how wretched you are, how pitiable and poor, how blind and naked" (Revelation 3:17). Are we generous enough and courageous enough to lean on one another, to be led by those whose vision is broader, to have our sight renewed by those whom we claim to have enlightened? Are we willing to exchange the gift of sight so that our common vision is enlarged and more clearly focused? "Even upon the servants and handmaids I will pour out my spirit" (Joel 3:1). We are instruments mutually of one another's enlightenment. Our redemption is in one another's hands.

We seek to be governed by a spirit of truth, and truth, we know, is light. Being guided into the truth can be a devastating experience. We will discover parts of ourselves we would rather ignore. We will begin to see where wrong and right and judgment lie (John 16:8), where the mediocre, the base, the counterfeit lie. And the question will always be: What will we do when the truth is revealed? Each such testing-time is a re-enactment of the desert experience that Jesus undertook. In those moments we can rely on our own power and influence, or we can acknowledge our weakness and our interconnectedness. We can attempt to prove our own theories and to work for our own ends, or we can open ourselves to the vast wisdom available to us. We can succumb to a single offer of glory or we can remain vulnerable and humble before life's gifts. One spirit will break the fragile bonds that unite us and will abort processes of healing, recreating, and making whole. The other will strengthen those bonds and lessen the forces of diminishment and alienation. "Every call of the Holy Spirit begins with a revelation of the bankruptcy of one's present, habitual mode of life, its tendency toward the death of one's spirit. That moment of awakening inevitably has to be a moment of anguish, of agony and of repentance, because it is only from the pain of awakening to the contradiction in one's life that the energy to change arises."[15]

Unlike the occasion of his baptism, Jesus was left alone in the desert to confront himself, his deepest spirit. Claimed by God in the first instance, Jesus claimed his own being in the second. We, too, need both experiences, the affirmation of our potential and the confrontation with our potential for evil. That is the inviolable interior of our spirit. All our relationships await the outcome of that personal crisis. In the crucible of truth, dreaded and resisted, we are purged. We come to learn who we really are, to whom we belong, and where it is that we are being sent.

TEACH US TO NUMBER OUR DAYS ARIGHT

"Seventy is the sum of our years, or eighty, if we are strong. Teach us to number our days aright that we may gain wisdom of heart" (Psalm 90:10, 12).

When I settled into East Anglia in 1986 to begin an extended stretch of ecumenical activity, I resolved to face anew the question of time and its potential tyranny. It was necessary above all in that rural existence to surrender some of the precision and freneticism that an urban environment imposes. Life in Norfolk is antithetical to digital clocks, strictly maintained appointment books, and nine-to-five workdays. It is clear what makes this so. One must respond to circumstances, to people and needs immediately at hand. Roosters crow at 4 a.m. Gardening is fitted into hours and days when weather permits. Trips to market towns or larger centers are planned carefully, and with irregular train schedules in mind. Electricity occasionally fails. Gifts of carrots and runner beans require an exchange of time and conversation. The local post office is more efficient in dispensing stories than stamps.

On the other hand, hours can pass undisturbed and uninterrupted. The expanse of field outside my window and the silent rows of wheat aided concentration and productivity. One works there in joint rhythm with life around: hours of daylight and darkness, moods of weather, haphazard timing of visitors. A stroll up the lane can provide fresh ideas as well as fresh air and exercise. Time lost in homely interaction can be regained in un-distracted hours and in freedom from the confusion of city life. East Anglia taught me something about freedom, freedom from the bondage of deadlines and artificial timetables, freedom to live and work in harmony with inner clocks and with measurements that are humane and sane and sensitive.

It also gave me the opportunity to insert myself in the stream of time, the ancient rhythms of settling and building, of planting and harvesting. The hedges that dissected and decorated my landscape had a history and a meaning that modern farming and develop-ment threaten. The cottage I lived in was once the home of crofters, those who worked the land for the gentry. In the grove nearby were the remains of a moat named in the Domesday Book. Roman legions once marched the roads that accommodated our yellow Volkswagen. And yet, there were signs of the new throughout the village. A younger population was restoring older dwellings and building new homes. Children planned and conducted a fund-raising event for flood victims in Bangladesh. U.S. air force planes droned incessantly in our vast skies. Even in rural Norfolk, life revealed the ambiguities of contemporary progress. We ourselves were calling people into a broader community of Christians, crossing age-old barriers of class and creed, connecting Norfolk to Britain and Britain to the rest of Europe and the world.

How to be free of time's tyranny while one is inserted into the stream of history and into the flow of change and growth—that is the paradoxical pleading of the psalmist: "Teach us to number our days aright that we may gain wisdom of heart." The past, wheth-er it be our personal past or our collective history, can be an in-sufferable burden, wearing away at our energies and pre-determining our perception of the present and the future. The pressures of time can rush in on us, controlling and de-humanizing us, so that we can neither breathe nor respond. At times we have all acted as robots, as programmed computers, heedless of personal limitations, insensitive to human factors. We have all been trained to move at the sound of the bell, to surpass yesterday's record, to stop and start with precision, to live in the shadow of the clock-tower.

Time ticks faster and faster and we try to keep up. That effort prevents us from dwelling in this moment, from moving through our days and weeks with an awareness of time's fullness, of time's connectedness, indeed of time's insignificance. We give time far more value that it deserves. We squander the only time we have in the process. This day will never return. This moment is the only one of its kind. "Teach us to number our days aright that we may gain wisdom of heart."

It is a plea that we might be open to time, to redeem the very meaning of time so that we might be free to have time "for everything under heaven," so that we might gain the blessings of a timed existence. In our search to find the connection between time and wisdom, we enter into the spirituality of time. We move from the question "What is time?" to "What time is it?"

THE PARADOX OF TIME

As an American, I perceive time as a commodity. Time is money. People in my world always seem to be in a hurry, even when they're not being paid by the hour. Cars rush past me on well-traveled streets trying to beat the traffic light ahead. People push their way through department stores and onto buses, determined to be first. Neighborhood shopping malls save time for avid customers. The status we've achieved is measured by the number of time-saving devices in our homes. Microwave ovens, self-recording videos, fast-food restaurants, drive-in banks, car telephones facilitate our freneticism. Whether one is in church, in a lawyer's office, at a meeting, or having lunch with a friend, one succumbs to the glance-at-the-watch syndrome. We are timed people, almost as if a delay might trigger a bomb, or our compact cars might turn into pumpkins if we are one minute late.

Americans, for one, have a peculiar fascination for records, especially for record-breaking. The weather is often reported in terms of records: the hottest, the driest, the windiest. A temperature of 98 seems somehow more bearable if we have managed to break a record for this particular day in July. Similarly with athletics: Who has begun the baseball season with the longest consecutive streak of wins, or, for that matter, losses? Who has the record for the number of successful times at bat? Who beat the existing record in the 100-meter dash or the 500-meter swimming competition? Children catch on quickly. I caught more fish than you did. I can jump rope faster than Tommy. The smallest toddler knows that the one who gets to the curb first is the victor.

We race and we record, we measure and we schedule time. Individual calendars, in purse or pocket, are indispensable. We don't know where we belong without them. If we lose some money, that's unfortunate, but if we lose those precious black books, we're desperate. Timing is crucial: timing your auto checkups, your cholesterol counts, your appearance at a party, your phone call to a prospective client, your coffee breaks, even your headaches. No time should be wasted, so we sit impatiently in doctors' offices, pace the floor at the airport, grumble when we find a line at the checkout counter. We set our clock radios for rising and spend the day keeping up with the pace we've set for ourselves, wondering why our food doesn't digest or we have high blood pressure, counting the days to our next holiday, racing our way to retirement. Convalescence is torture, retirement is a crisis, the prospect of aging and immobility is terrifying. "Teach us to number our days aright that we may gain wisdom of heart."

Occasionally we catch glimpses of life's fleetingness, of inevitable limitations, of the foolishness of our frenzied strides. We confess our compulsiveness about time and resolve to live at a more human pace, at least while the stitches are still mending or our children require extra attention. We sense that ultimately we are losers in this battle against time and aging and mortality. We recognize our need for something lasting, our yearning to belong to something eternal, until the phone rings or the lights beckon and we are off again to another competition with the clock.

The paradox of this stop-start existence is that we all spend ample proportions of our time in that helpless activity called Waiting. Life, in some sense, is waiting. We wait for our first tooth, our first words and steps. We wait for school to finish and school to commence, for that bicycle and that camping trip. We wait for birthdays and Christmas. When they have passed, we wait for something else—the arrival of the mail, the visit of a friend, the next trip abroad. We worry while we wait: the report of medical tests, our income taxes, a verdict on a case, a pending confrontation. We wait while we heal, while a dream is born, while a loved one dies. Is it true that we are willing to wait for what we love?

We accept waiting as necessary for human beings. We steel ourselves, resign ourselves, passively put up with the phenomenon we can't control or eliminate. Only rarely do we perceive the value of waiting, its potential for taming us and slowing us down, its ability to shift our perspective from doing to receiving, from self-sufficiency to creaturehood, from dominance to vulnerability. Waiting has the capacity to humanize us, to diminish our need to control and manipulate, to unleash in us the forces of creativity and the powers of wisdom. Waiting opens us to time.

Those with a feminine spirit are perhaps more attuned to the benefits of waiting. Childbearing, physical cycles, vigils of all sorts teach lasting lessons of tenderness and sensitivity. Slowly and gradually experiences like the one described by Frederick Buechner make their mark on our restless, urgent spirits:

> On a winter night you are waiting for somebody who is journeying home to you. The roads are icy, and the radio has been full of accident reports. There comes a point where you can't bear just to sit there any longer; you go stand at the window to watch for the lights of cars. But one after another, the cars all pass by and continue up the hill out of sight. An hour late becomes an hour and a half, two hours late. You try to find something to take your mind off it, but there's too much more of you involved by now than just your mind, and you can feel your face grow gray with waiting.[1]

"This focused attentiveness of waiting is not opposed to action. It is one way women's spirituality offers for bridging the gap between being and doing."[2] Not for a moment do we think passive the women who waited during the Gulf War, or the women who wait still at Greenham Common, or those who tend the dying in hospices. We begin to understand and to know solidarity with the relatives of hostages, the wives and mothers of policemen, those who risk the perils of fishing and mining to earn a livelihood. We begin to relate to a God who waits for a prodigal child, for a wayward people, throughout the climb to Calvary; to a God who accompanies those who sleep rough night after night, those who migrate in search of food, those whose final home is a refugee camp. We begin to appreciate the seasonal waitings of the church calendar: Lent, Advent, times of vigil. Time to absorb, to prepare, to repent.

Time is a mystery for most of us. Anticipation, joy, fullness one moment, and suspense, fear, dread the next. Time passes quickly when we are engrossed, when all is well. Time halts when worry and pain invade our being and clog our imagination and hope. In fact, time exists according to our moods and feelings. Either we are bored and amass time, anxious and struggling with it, searching and therefore needing it, or delighting in something and trying to clasp it. Time is elastic and elusive. An hour with someone we love is but a moment. It slips through our embrace and disappears like light in the sky once the sun dips below the horizon.

On the other hand, an hour is tortuously long when we await word of someone's safety or when we await results of a close election. I recently took a driving test for a British license. I was amazed and horrified how time clamped my spirit that last hour before my examiner appeared and the test got underway. Time is qualitative, subjective, intensely personal. A three-month separation can be an eternity. Deadlines pounce when we are pressured from within and without. For me the last moments before a public speech, the few seconds I wait to hear the doctor's verdict, the last bit of time before the plane touches ground, are interminable. But I don't even notice time when I am immersed in writing, or hiking in the mountains, or engaged in a gripping conversation.

Time is an enemy for some. For those who are lonely or depressed, with time on their hands, it is an endless stretch of nothingness and non-activity. Companionship, of whatever sort, converts time into an ally. It takes so much longer to live a day when there are no voices, no responses, no exchange. Meaningless activity turns time into a tyrant. Repetition and monotony exaggerate the slow ticking of hours and days. For those oppressed by pressures and demands, time is an obstacle. Try using a key in a lock when nervous or hurrying across town to make an appointment when traffic is heavy. We speak of beating the clock, of being governed by time, of killing time. We even play games against the backdrop of a timer. Time becomes an object, a foe, and we are its victims or its opponents. Life becomes a battlefield or a prison. We are defeated and debilitated by time.

Humanly speaking, time catches up with us. "Once upon a time" is only for fairy tales. In reality, it is always Now. And we know not the day or the hour.

Time has a freakish dimension. One moment life is regular and ordinary. Then suddenly everything is different. An accident and one is never the same again. A tragedy and life is completely reversed. "Where is there a person whose sense of time has not been revolutionized by a particular crucial event?...Any profound conversion involves a transformation of calendar as much as of character; it may be described as the receiving of a new, inner chronometer, the adopting of a new calendar. And with a shift in the sense of time, our whole universe shifts into new focus."[3]

Each time we turn on the TV news, we know that somewhere for someone life will have stopped and reality will have taken a desperate course. We keep one ear to our radios to be assured that our world is still intact, that time has not disrupted our existence. We wake each morning relieved, if not grateful, that we have survived to see another day. We recognize the poignancy in all our good-byes, for one of them will be final. "Teach us to number our days aright that we might gain wisdom of heart."

KAIROS TIME

One of my personal goals in life is to become free enough and flexible enough to find time for those things that are important to me. So often we name priorities, but our actual behavior betrays us. Ecclesiastes tells us there is an appointed time for everything. We dismiss this as a bit of fatalism. There isn't a time for every affair under heaven. Many things are ill-timed and some events shouldn't happen at all. And yet we mean something similar when we speak of "kairos," the moment of grace, of choice, of the convergence of history and personal destiny.

Recognizing the crucial points in our lives and times requires diligent discernment—when to plant the seeds of truth or of confidence, when to uproot destructive habits in our own systems or destructive systems in our societies, when to rage over the horrors of human cruelty, when to mourn the deadliness that penetrates our universe and our communities, when to celebrate the feasts of life, when to seek new horizons and risk new ventures, when to let go and transfer responsibility to other or younger hands, when to be silent and watchful and withhold judgment, when to speak words of encouragement or of criticism—to know what time it is!

At Cana, Jesus said bluntly: "My time has not yet come." It was not the occasion to reveal himself, to expose a ministry that was yet too vulnerable. Timing was of utmost importance to Jesus. He knew when a crowd's adulation was premature and fickle, and he slipped away. There are times to fast, he proposed, and times to be angry, times to disobey and times to go apart. Jesus' life was one of discernment, always available to the sinner, the one in need, and always protective of his priorities. Jesus did not have time for idle gossip or the insincere or for vain publicity or unnecessary compromise. Be alert, be ready for that unexpected moment of grace and of choice, he advised his disciples who were so inept at reading the signs of their times. Be open to the time at hand!

It is good for us to dwell among creation and to study its rhythms. Trees know the time of budding and the time of baring. The moon moves through its cycles with ease and constancy. Coconuts and apples fall from their heights when the time is right, and even the ripe blackberry responds easily to plucking fingers. Those cultures that have long kept nature's secrets teach us who are blind and clumsy and exploitative. In contrast to the greed of today's agribusiness, primal peoples and ordinary farmers understand the importance of fallow fields and the timing of their restoration. Stories are told of Indian hermits who know it is time for them to become wandering, begging *sanyasis* and of the American Indian grandmother who knows death will come once she has completed her weaving.

Time "connects" us. We are where we came from. Our past experiences have formed us. Our roots and our history have been the soil from which our creative ideas and fruitful relationships have grown. Our memories give us an identity. Our reading of the past helps define our purpose and our direction. We are part of a process, a procession. It is a glorious unfolding, as well as a record of blemishes and detours. We are paving the way for future generations. Our hopes are the framework for their freedoms and opportunities. It is in this context that we then make our contribution, invest our talents. "Grant us a clear vision, that in this hour of our history we may see the horizon and know the way on which your kingdom comes to us."[4]

"Now is the acceptable time." The prophet John pronounced it and prophets in every age have reiterated it. "If today you hear God's voice, harden not your hearts." Things don't have to be the way they are. Frances Cabrini, Lanzo del Vasto, Helen Caldicott, Shanti Solomon, George Fox, and Franz Jagerstatter: Each seized the moment and sowed seeds for a more acceptable future.

Now is the time for repentance and responsibility. It is the time for churches to heal their history and to make the mission that unites them their priority. It is the time for communities to reach out to those at the margins and to become marginal, if necessary, in their commitment to justice. Now is the time of obedience, of reconciliation, of risk—and it is non-transferable. "I call heaven and earth today to witness against you. I have set before you life and death, the blessing and the curse. Choose life" (Deuteronomy 30:19). "The demand of God in the present moment," says Paul Minear, "is not hedged about with qualifications concerning the limited response which the conditions of life make possible: It is always clear, uncompromising, absolute, as a call to total obedience."[5]

Choosing calls for action, not discussion, or postponement, or even meditation. Obedience is concrete and now. Every present moment is an opportunity. "I was hungry and you...I was away from home...I was ill and in prison and you..." (Matthew 25:35ff). "For three years now I have come in search of fruit on this fig tree and found none. Cut it down. Why should it clutter up the ground?" (Luke 13:7). In the words of a friend, what do we do if God is hungry for figs at the wrong season of the year?[6]

There was a moment in 1981 at a mission conference in Chicago when I met a stranger. The ensuing journey we have shared has turned my life upside down and re-formed many of my views and values. Not to live in the present moment is to risk losing the way. Not to be open to the persons who are given us or to read the message in today's events is to jeopardize the course of our pilgrimage. To live too much in the past and its regrets is to be distracted from the urgent agenda of this hour. To ignore our own mortality and to entrust important tasks to an unknown future is to be deluded. We may think a child's question trivial in the light of our professional agendas. We may think a specific request negligible compared to our sophisticated schedules. A single sign is obscure and ambiguous next to our carefully planned routes.

But so was the plight of the man who fell among robbers a nuisance to the Levite and an inconvenience to the priest. We can rationalize about the statistics we gather and report and about the beggars we pass on our trips to the city. We can lament at the end of a busy day how stretched we were and how hard we worked. We can carry yesterday's burdens as baggage or procrastinate for a time. The stars will continue to shine and the budding daffodils will still poke their way into our gardens. Even our children will find explanations somewhere, and someone else will notice the "sign." But we are in danger of becoming blind and deaf, insensitive and abstract. We may give others stones when they ask for bread. We may forego the only opportunity we have to know life's intimacy, its immediacy, its superabundance. "I have seen the sun break through to illuminate a small field for a while, and gone my way and forgotten it. But that was the pearl of great price...."[7]

TAKING AND GIVING TIME

A spirituality of time must have something to do with give and take. In Norfolk, I knew it was important to take time to talk with neighbors, to walk the lane, to welcome the first snowdrop, to pause at sunset. What we take time for reveals our priorities. I see again the wisdom of the horarium that was the framework for monastic life. It ensured that time would be taken for prayer, for solitude, for manual labor, for leisure. I marveled recently as I rode a London subway. It was evening rush hour and a young businessman stood in the crowded carriage clutching a hand-strap, his briefcase between his feet and in his free hand an open book. He was taking time to read, noise and confusion not-withstanding.

What matters at the end is what really matters, a wise person has said. Will we regret not taking time for specific people in our lives: our children, our parents, young people, old friends? For not taking time to study that favorite subject, to grow in prayer and reflection, to review our hectic careers and the pace of our comings and goings? It is the time you spent on your rose, said the little Prince, that mattered. Some of life's deepest and most startling lessons emerge from experiences that take time: the sow-ing and tending of a garden, the mending of a broken leg or a broken heart, the mastering of a new language, the overcoming of one of our unfreedoms.

And the second question: To what do we *give* time? The answer to that question reveals the balancing of our inner and outer worlds. It implies a willingness, a wholeheartedness. We are to *give* time, not begrudge it or offer it stintingly. Not to give it is to waste it or to hoard it. We can be present, and not just physically, to those with whom we work, to the task at hand. What we do is worth doing and doing well. The gift of time surpasses other gifts. Giving time is giving self, the best of self. A shepherd has need to give little else. Likewise a teacher, a pastor, a social worker. Who will keep watch over this green earth of ours, these children en-trusted to us, over the precious resources of prairie and forest, ex-cept those who give time to them? Who will guard that justice is done to those who are oppressed, unemployed, to those who are immigrant or disabled, except those who give time to it? We give time to what is fragile and dear and irreplaceable. I know why a young woman in my life lights up when I offer her a Kristy-day. It is her time, a time for her to be honored and appreciated.

A spirituality of time is characterized by vigilance. "We must do the deeds of the one who sent us while it is day" (John 9:4). There is still time to be reconciled with those who are alienated. Time to begin the slow tasks of purifying our rivers and preserving our air. Time to reverse the nuclear nonsense with which we have defended ourselves. Time to take care of our health. Time to save our drug-ridden and despairing inner cities. "Over the bleached bones of numerous civilizations," said Martin Luther King, "are written the pathetic words: Too late. If we do not act, we shall surely be dragged down the dark corridors of time reserved for those who possess power without compassion, might without morality, and strength without sight."[8]

Finally, a spirituality of time must keep us mindful of our own temporality. "Our days are like those of grass, like a flower of the field we bloom. The wind sweeps over us and we are gone" (Psalm 103:15-16). The time we have is a treasure, but it is on loan. It will pass quickly. I think of friends who were alive a year ago and whose company I no longer enjoy. I think of those who lost their lives escaping from East Germany just years or months before the wall came down. We are made conscious of our fragility in such terrible and shocking ways. A flood in Asia claims tens of thousands of lives in one swoop. A school girl doesn't return from school and her body is found in the river. A child is abused once too often. An auto accident ends the lives of an entire family while on vacation.

Occasionally we are graced with a glimpse of eternity: love that is so deep that death cannot diminish it, solemn rites of celebration that lift us into the company of all the saints who have preceded us, glorious moments of star-filled skies, majestic mountains, vast seas, or delicate features of babies. These are moments when one feels a pervading peace with all around, a harmony in the hills and heathers, a unity of breath and strength and hope. "God has put the timeless into their hearts" (Ecclesiastes 3:11).

I once attended a musical performance led by a black cast. In an inimitable way, they involved us all in the music and movement. There was a refrain: *You're in the Right Place at the Right Time*. As we chanted it, we turned to our neighbors, right and left, ahead and behind, and placed one hand on the hand of another. Together we clapped it out: *You're in the Right Place at the Right Time*. It summarizes vocation. And Kairos.

We are called again and again into the dance of life, its simple rhythms and its complex movements. The tempo changes, like the flow of a river. Each moment brings its own promise and its own demands. Some moments we *take*, for nourishment and growth. And some we *give*, generously and graciously. Each moment offers its own wisdom. Each moment, if we are open to it, is the time of God's visitation.

CHAPTER THREE

GO FORTH TO A LAND I WILL SHOW YOU

"Leave your country, your family, and your parents' house, for the land I will show you" (Genesis 12:1).

I am amazed and sometimes amused at the process the British use to "place" one another. It is a relic of the full-blown class system. When you meet someone for the first time, you might engage in a little skirmish of queries and responses seeking the "key": a common place or school or name or experience. My accent, of course, gives me away, but people nonetheless want to ferret out who I am: my background, my profession, my qualifications. "What is your place?" is the underlying question.

Living in the United Kingdom has meant learning a new geography, inner and outer, everything from road routes to the topography of church institutions. I still confuse directions, expecting the train to London to arrive on the opposite track. Recognizing whether a city being mentioned is northwest or southeast is a challenge. Watching television is a course in civics, culture, economics, and language. I slowly absorb the parliamentary system, the national health service, the world of building societies, and the idiosyncrasies of the royal family. I am acquiring a new set of acronyms, from ACTS to VAT. It is similar in my ecumenical explorations. Understanding the various religious traditions in a British context demands a suspension of previously held perceptions. Church and state in the United Kingdom are in-

terconnected in ways undreamed of in the United States. Roman
Catholics are a minority church, with resulting implications. The
effects of the Reformation are visible, and one experiences emotional as well as theological residues. Parish life, liturgy, evangel-
ism, social responsibility have their peculiarly British contours.

Within, too, there is a process of redefining and relocating. I
find that our common language is not always common. My allu-
sions or interpretations can be missed or misunderstood. My relationships must necessarily shift as I meet new people and col-
laborate with new groups. My inner map changes from familiar
circles to ever enlarging and more temporary friendships. I probe
some of the deeper meanings of *stranger* and *outsider* and *newcom-
er*. I am forced to decide what the rocks and the roots are that
transcend geography. In many ways, I walk less surely, more
observant of signposts, more conscious of my blind spots, less
confident in my map-reading skills. I am finding my way in a
new world.

WHERE DO WE BELONG?

To be human is to be placed. We occupy a particular corner of the
earth, and it plays a significant role in our shaping and our
outlook. "He shall be called a Nazarean." That meant something
to the Jews of Jesus' day. Can anything good come from Naz-
areth? In former times it was natural to identify oneself by one's
geography: Paul of Tarsus, Julian of Norwich, Teresa of Avila.
Wordsworth's name is still one with the Lake District, Shakespeare's with Stratford, Dickens's with London.

Our places of residence, our family homesteads, even our countries of birth are our larger selves. We identify with them, so
much so that a criticism of America is often taken as a negative
remark about me. In a special way we take responsibility for the
delights and the dilemmas of our particular town or nation. Milwaukee's parks and lakefront, its mayor, its bishop, will always
be *my* parks, *my* mayor, *my* bishop.

In Europe it is common to name one's house, and the name one
chooses often reveals something of the owner's personality. Calling cards are symbols of our eagerness to be located, as are the

plethora of directories we produce. We insist even on locating God, up there, in heaven, in church. Indeed, in so doing, we make a theological statement.

Our need to locate extends beyond life itself. Bodies must be brought home for burial. Grief is doubled when the body of a loved one cannot be found. We think of the intense agony of the wives and children of the men who died on the Piper Alpha oil rig. Some bodies have never been recovered. Cemeteries are often a place of pilgrimage for families and friends.

Place makes us somebody. We are nobody if we have no address, no home town. It is the plight of so many in our world today: the homeless, refugees, the displaced. Even children need a place of their own: a shelf, a drawer, a corner of the room. Most of us fall into the habit of claiming our place: of work, our chair, our pew. It gives us freedom and privacy, security and identity. When we have no place of our own, we experience poverty. "The worst of poverty—today at any rate—the most galling and most difficult thing to bear, is that it makes it almost impossible for one to be alone."[1] Poverty confiscates privacy and the luxury of space.

Place means belonging. If we are away from our place, we are missed. If we are displaced, we become disoriented. The tragedy of the loss of land: the family farm, Palestinian resettlements, the crofters of Scotland, migration in Africa, is that the very identity of those who dwelt there goes with it. Without roots, we are stripped of part of our humanity. Similarly, we become a people when we share a place. Places unite us and form us into a community. Often when I say Geneva or Guelph or Windermere or St. Ben's, I am naming a *people* of whom I am part. It is the staff of the World Council of Churches who are Geneva to me, the ecumenical groups with whom we met that constitute Guelph, the retreatants who are Windermere, and the family of street persons, friends, and co-ministers who are St. Ben's. More and more of us seek global citizenship. More and more of us view creation as that largest, most sacred community to which we belong.

Our human need to belong has spiritual implications. We are to grow where we are planted. We grow best in an environment that suits us, not too comfortable, not too harsh. The ground we stand on is holy. The reign of God is in our midst. But as Christians it is equally imperative that we know ourselves as pilgrims, wayfarers, sojourners in a foreign land. Gabriel Marcel once described human existence as "wayfaring," *homo viator*. Our appearances on the human stage are numbered, Shakespeare tells us. We are merely players; we have our exits and our entrances.[2] We have no permanent abode. We are all in exile. "Man [sic] has something in him which transcends ordinary terrestrial life and is restless if confined to it."[3] Chardin says: "We are cosmic beings with cosmic longings."[4]

"Leave this place," God said to Adam and Eve in Eden. "Go forth to a land I will show you," God spoke to Abraham and Sarah. "Lead my people out of Egypt," God commanded Moses. The Exodus is the symbol of our Christian pilgrimage. The historical books of the Old Testament follow the movements of the people of Israel, from region to region, in and out of slavery and captivity, in good times and bad. "Whenever the cloud rose, the Israelites would set out on their journey...whereas at night, fire was seen in the cloud by the whole house of Israel in all the stages of their journey" (Exodus 40:38). And the psalmist echoes their experience: "The Lord will guard your coming and your going both now and forever" (Psalm 121:8).

The theme resumes in the New Testament. Mary set out in haste to travel to her cousin Elizabeth. Joseph and Mary were enroute to Bethlehem when Jesus' birth took them unprepared. Where do you stay? was the first apostles' way of asking Jesus a whole range of questions. Jesus' ministry was a pilgrimage, into the desert, from village to village, across borders into Samaria and Judea and, ultimately, to Jerusalem. Leave your nets, Jesus said, leave your homes and even your dead, leave behind the thought of possessions and security. The Human One has nowhere to lay his head. Take up your cross and follow me. And later: Go into the whole world with the message of the Gospel. Become a pilgrim people, renew the world through which you move. Remain free to follow your migrant leader.

Mobility is a fact of life for most of us. We expect to pack up periodically. We know that our roots cannot be only physical. We try to remember that the mission that occupies us belongs to God and not to us. The commonwealth we are building is not in our own name. For me personally becoming a pilgrim in deed and in truth is a gradual process. I have loved the homes in which I have dwelt and I feel a personal tearing when I leave a place that has become hallowed by familiar routines, by homely efforts to care for it, and by memories of visitors and celebrations. I am not a "collector" in any strong sense, but I do like to have easy access to my books and my files. All those little gifts and mementoes that speak to me of days in India or remind me of distant friends, where are they?

Keenest of all, who are my people? As my life becomes more and more a series of farewells and reunions, family members grow up and some become strangers. Friends are disappointed by my continued absence. I miss out on special events: weddings and births, jubilees and community celebrations. My very fidelity to family and community becomes suspect. And yet, my heart is set on the pilgrimage. Exact details about the stripping and letting go still to come are not available. Today it may be questions of health, tomorrow a wrenching of heart. I am constantly surprised at the direction and the depth of the journey. I have not yet mastered the meaning of Blake's words:

> [She] who binds to [herself] a joy
> Does the winged life destroy;
> But [she] who kisses the joy as it flies
> Lives in eternity's sunrise.[5]

Places, no matter their size or location, can be prisons. Some of our churches and political institutions are narrow and confining. Even countries as vast as the United States can be insular and excommunicating in their outlook. As I have been nourished by a world church, I have felt an increased claustrophobia in at least some dimensions of Roman Catholicism. As I have tasted of other cultures, I find aspects of my own native culture tasteless and boring. The door of our houses must be left ajar. The winds of curiosity must be allowed to blow through. We know how our relationships can become stale and stunted without enough stimulation and outreach. Our work can become dull if it is not balanced by leisure and opportunities for growth. It is the difference between a swamp and a fresh-water lake. The latter depends on a current flowing in and channels for the outflow. So it is with whatever place we occupy. If it is sealed off, our life atrophies and stagnates. On the other hand, actual prisons have the potential for liberation. We have witnessed the effect of prison on Nelson Mandela, Karl Gaspar, Vaclav Havel, and others.

The vocation of disciples today is to become global Christians. The world is our place, our home, our parish. Some of us have been privileged to travel. Ours is a grave responsibility: to translate our insights into new attitudes, to communicate the lessons we have imbibed, to be bridge builders for those who fear or who cast stones. All of us have access to the media. We are bombarded with far more information than we can absorb. But we have a responsibility to expand our horizons and to stretch our spirits to include those most remote from us and to adopt those most neglected. Geography is a good beginning for serious-minded Christians. Knowing one another and establishing a relationship is basic to building community, whether local or international, geopolitical or religious. World mission presumes world geography.

Travel and contact with other cultures changes how we see ourselves. They serve a relativizing purpose. Our pinpoint on the map becomes one of a multitude rather than the center of the universe. We begin to understand the ways in which we are interrelated and interdependent. We begin to take responsibility for other parts of the world that are affected by our economic and foreign policies and that affect us in turn by their shared resources and cultural exchange. We recognize opportunities to complement one another, to gift one another, to extend our family memories. Things done differently in other places are not done incorrectly. Our systems of education and food preparation and law-making are not better than others. Absolutes are challenged, differences are integrated, plurality and diversity become values.

Becoming global Christians affects our prayer, our manner of intercession, our style of worship, our understanding of church.

We ask new questions about the implications of our lifestyle. Our own privations are put in perspective. Our very concept of mission is enlarged and enriched. Ecumenism becomes natural. Justice and peace become essential ingredients of every ministry. Partnership with the earth includes all the fragile links we have with water and air, with future generations. We sing the praises of creation by using the fruits of the earth sparingly and by honoring earth's limitations. We sing the songs of Zion by restoring land to those who cherish it, freedom to those oppressed, a homeplace to those exiled and refugeed.

"By acknowledging themselves to be strangers and foreigners upon the earth, they showed that they were seeking a homeland" (Hebrews 11:13-14). Mindful of the sacred ground that nourishes us, marveling that "it is good for us to be here," we Christians are still homesick for that promised land. Our present home is a place of exile. The place to which we belong is being built within, in faithful hearts, in lives where justice is the foundation, in efforts to imitate the breadth and depth and length and height of Christ's love. Allegiance to that country requires struggle and resistance. "Put on the armor of God...wear truth around your waist, justice as your breastplate and zeal on your feet" (Ephesians 6:14-15).

INNER AND OUTER SPACE

As the human spaces close that separate us geographically, linguistically, and ideologically, we come face to face with the necessity of preserving and expanding *inner* space. The more we open ourselves to the realities, joys, and griefs of a global village, the more we desperately need discerning hearts to filter and prioritize. As our technology and our future draw us into outer space with its mysteries and thresholds, we seek a balance with the journey inward, to the deep places of integrity. As we grow more and more overcrowded, physically and psychically, we yearn for inner freedom and inner silence to rehabilitate and to re-establish harmony. Our western societies in particular are more adept at conquering and cultivating outer space than at fostering inner resources. We train ourselves to cope with the pace of modern life, but we neglect the hunger of the human spirit for unity within.

It was easy to regain the image of space in East Anglia. My overall impression was openness and breathing room. We all need those places of discovery, our vast plains or our mountains of transfiguration. I need the Jura Mountains, even my memories of them, because visiting there restores some of the exhilaration of climbing and of moving cross-country on skis. We need the sea to restore our perspective: My boat is so tiny and the ocean so vast. We need the desert to surface our fears and to confront our own shadows. We need the open roads to invite us to move onward and to enjoy our freedoms.

Native Americans and Buddhists, among others, teach us the significance of the space that surrounds us. In the words of a Native American prayer:

Weave for us a garment of brightness
May the warp be the white light of morning
May the fringes be the falling rain
May the borders be the standing rainbow
Weave for us a garment of brightness
That we may walk fittingly where birds sing
That we may walk fittingly where grass is green
O our mother the earth, O our father the sky.[6]

I have never forgotten the lesson a Buddhist once voiced. When you walk, be aware of those who walk alongside you, behind you, before you, of those on whose efforts you now stand. We are surrounded, says the writer of Hebrews, by a cloud of witnesses.

Some of us would like to confine and limit God. People commonly cast a glance upward when they refer to the Transcendent, or speak of "heaven" as God's abode. We learned well the transcendent quality of God, but we are less at home with God's immanence. People in the past have found themselves judged heretical. But in our more creation-centered spiritualities, we are opting to remove the boundaries enclosing God. We know God through Jesus, and Jesus was an earthling. God is here in our midst, going before us, following us, leading us, calling us. God is

within us and every other creature, in our histories and our crea-
tions. God is in the seasons and cycles, in the wind's whisper and
the cataract's roar. God is in the mighty oak and in the shyest
primrose. God's voice and gesture are cloaked in a myriad of messages and signs.

Changes occur as the space around us and within us opens up,
and especially as the space between us becomes sacred. We
claim—and need—less. We shepherd more faithfully. We rely
more on the secrets of nature and the assurance of our friendships. We are less insecure, we have less to clutch and to protect.
We are more open and tolerant. Our identity has enlarged.

This is the threshold of a spirituality of place. This is the entrance to the paradox of our wayfaring and our belonging, our at-
tachments and our open hands, our solitude and our common
life. We have to find the way in this world of inner and outer
space, of rhythms of coming and going, of experiences of breadth
and of depth. "Go alone into your chamber," Jesus advised those
who would pray and discern. It is the proper place for prayer.
Dwell there. "Be still and see that I am God." The mystics are the
map makers of this inner landscape. But so are the natural mystics: Annie Dillard, Jacques Cousteau, Wendell Berry, Kathleen
Raine, Nikos Kazantzakis. And the mystics of traditions less familiar to us: Angelus Silesius, Susan Griffin, Martin Buber, Thich
Nhat Hanh.

Once we have inhabited an inner space, we will find that it is
inviolable. In the image of James Clavell's *Shogun*, we can build
there an eight-fold fence. And, when necessary, we can withdraw
into the third or fourth enclosure. Nothing can penetrate us there,
not even insults and ill treatment. We have the testimonies of
modern witnesses that this has been the case. "One of the most
wonderful discoveries which I have made in this pilgrimage of
my life is that there comes a moment when you don't look for a
reward any longer...What is of importance is your experience of
life, of an inner peace, of a strength of faith...an inner deep conviction of the power of truth and of love."[7] "I may face deprivation and cruelty the likes of which I cannot imagine even in my
wildest fantasies. Yet all this is as nothing compared to the

immeasurable expanse of my faith in God and my inner receptiveness."[8] Knowing that we have such a dwelling place, we are able to venture forth into danger. When we are centered within, we are capable of presence and of communion.

John Dunne summarized the effects of this colonization of inner space:

> It is not that I am unable to return to my own journey or to personal religion or to my own particular way in life. It is rather that my journey has become the journey together, my religion has become that of the poor, and my way has become that of the universal heart's desire. My own road disappears now into the human road. To act, nevertheless, I must travel the journey together as my own journey, live the religion of the poor as personal religion, walk the universal way as my way.[9]

The story is told of Elzéard Bouffier. He had lost his wife and son and farm. He had withdrawn into the foothills of the Alps where he lived alone with his dog. It was his belief that the surrounding area was dying for lack of trees. Virtually every day of his life for the next thirty years, without mechanical assistance, Elzéard Bouffier planted trees: oaks, beeches, birches. Slowly, year by year, the land was transformed. Water began to flow again in the brooks. The wind scattered seeds. Grasses grew, and meadows, and flowers. Entire forests appeared where there had been only barren land. Once again the area was alive: the sound of children laughing, the activities of farming, the building of human community. Elzéard Bouffier converted a wasteland into a garden. He did it over many years, by painstaking and monotonous toil. He "knew his place." He loved his place into life. He shepherded creation until it was fruitful. In the words of the storyteller, his was "a magnificent generosity."[10]

The story is told in Mark's gospel of Simon and the others searching for Jesus, who had escaped at dawn to a quiet place to pray. Confronted by the queries of his disciples, Jesus answered: "Let us move on to the neighboring villages so that I may proclaim the good news there also. That is what I have come to do" (Mark 1:28). Jesus' place was "on the move," wherever there was brokenness and need.

It is that assurance of direction, that commitment to the specific task given each of us, that should characterize a follower of Jesus. Whatever our particular plot of land, we are to cultivate it. Whatever our particular skill and vision, we are to maximize it. Like Elzéard Bouffier, we are to live with a magnificent generosity. Like Jesus, we are to spend ourselves and then move on to the next acre. That is what we have been sent to do, to make a garden where there is wasteland, to rebuild ancient ruins, to accompany the exiled (including our own lost selves) back to their native lands, to proclaim good news to our fellow travelers, to be at home in every place, and never at home until God's commonwealth is established.

DOUBT NO LONGER, BUT BELIEVE

"I will not believe until I have put my fingers into the place of the nails and my hand into his side" (John 20:25).

Thomas spoke for all of us who refuse to take on faith what others would have us believe. Faith by osmosis is too easy—born into it, spoon-fed it, blind faith. It was in the atmosphere when I was a novice in the 1950s. Don't question, just obey. Part of the plan of holiness was to test the ability of the novice to suspend personal will and thought in favor of submission to authority, to surrender logic and common sense in favor of humiliation or even absurdity. And the models held up to us were those who complied.

But that phenomenon was only a piece of the mosaic of pre-Vatican II Roman Catholicism. Obedience was *the* virtue, obedience "upwards," laity to priest, priests to bishops, bishops to pope, and within that system, novices to superiors. Docility and humility (false, perhaps) were the daughter-virtues. I once got out of my bed at midnight to go with an older nun to a train station to meet someone who never arrived and whose identity I didn't dare ask. We returned in silence after a couple of hours' wait at Amtrak. I never received an explanation.

My novice director once asked me what size shoe I wore. Then she bade me bring her my best pair. I didn't see them for months. When I finally dredged up courage to ask for a new pair, she went to a cupboard and produced my own "best pair," now wrapped in brown paper. I surmised only that a novice who left the convent wore them home and mailed them back. Maybe her own shoes were deemed too disgraceful to leave in. I asked no questions.

Such novitiate stories could fill volumes. My counterparts in parishes and seminaries and marriage courses could match them. Don't upset the pastor. Your husband shouldn't mistreat you, but don't leave him. It must be God's will that you have cancer. Your reward for your perseverance will come later. Above all, don't question the catechism, or the law, or the traditional way of doing things. Good Catholics accept the church's mind.

Even within those pressures, there were moments when I doubted. When my four-month-old nephew was brought on visiting day I had to break the rules to hold him, behind the convent garden bushes. It was supposedly too great a temptation to celibacy to cuddle a baby. Doubts came when I was scolded and punished for being late for a duty because I had gone to chapel to pray after receiving the disturbing news that my niece had contracted meningitis. The human and the holy were often in conflict in those days. Of course I wanted to be holy, so I had to doubt the importance and the value of being human.

A doubt-free existence can only result in an immature mind. Can children who never rebel ever become independent? We know there are still plenty of Christians who fear their doubts, deny them, refuse to ask questions, believe blindly, and remain immature in their faith. There is another side, of course. Doubts can also paralyze us, prevent us from acting or growing. They can become excuses for our inertia, our lack of commitment.

For most people, doubts are inevitable and healthy. We may have doubts about our own capabilities, our lovableness, doubts about the veracity of someone we trusted, doubts about God, life after death, the meaning of suffering, doubts regarding authority, relationships, decisions already made. Times when we have had to suspend belief in ourselves, a loved one, an authority figure, in God, are times when we are opened to a new dimension of human life. We are pushed out of the safe and the comforting into a vacuum. We are alone in our confusion and uncertainty. Maybe my professors or advisers are wrong. What if God is only an idea we've been taught? If I make this decision, will it "shrink" me? Should I throw caution to the wind and risk this step into the unknown?

DOUBTING, FOR LIFE'S SAKE

I doubted that the decision to send me to study philosophy, first an M.A., then a Ph.D., was a right decision. I suspected that it was because of my consistently good grades in undergraduate studies that they picked me out of a file, so to speak. Certainly I wasn't consulted. I found myself in a Jesuit university, on my way through ancient, medieval, and modern philosophy, reading Aristotle and Aquinas, Kant and Gilson. Snatched out of the high school in which I had begun to establish myself as a teacher, I was now held captive in stuffy seminar rooms, wrestling with systems of thought that I was never quite sure I understood. In my innocence I got good grades. How did I manage to fool everyone? Did some people actually know what they were talking about? Was it all a mistake? Was it God's will (as my superiors told me every time I raised the issue)?

At that time, in that university, philosophy was a man's world. Scholastic philosophy was the order of the day. What did all this have to do with my life? I had wanted to teach children. I spent one entire year writing a dissertation about God: God and I in a little noisy elevator shaft on the fourth floor of a residence hall. What did it mean? I doubted—a lot—but I was obedient.

Did I even take note of that one humorous moment in those four years? I had arrived on the campus far in advance of the start of my dissertation orals. I sat on a bench outdoors, rigidly nervous, still cramming. Just as I decided it was time to approach the trial chamber, a bird overhead dumped a load on my black veil (I was still in habit). There was just enough time to undress and wash the stain before my auspicious professors escorted me into the room of judgment. A lucky omen, some would say. A final blow, I thought.

The doubts grew when, post-Ph.D., I got into my own classroom. No matter how much I adapted the syllabus, introduced other disciplines into my course, like novels, poetry, and political essays, I still found this immense gap between the lives of my 19-year-old students and the systematic, scholastic philosophy I was supposed to teach. It was so neat and tidy, so abstract, so logical, so comprehensive. Their lives, and mine actually, were so concrete, so chaotic, so much in crisis. They had real questions about love and sex and suffering and the future, and so did I. I doubted that the ethics and metaphysics textbooks were very helpful to them. I doubted that my Ph.D. qualified me to open up their minds to the wisdom and beauty and fragility of life around them. I doubted that academia was the place where I was meant to be. I felt alone in wanting students to enjoy philosophy, to probe their own questions and experiences, alone in the accusations that hinted I was misleading them, failing to uphold the standards of the department. Was I right to cast into doubt the validity and relevancy of syllabi and term papers and the very comprehensiveness of Thomistic thought? Was it more important that they absorb what others long ago thought rather than learn to think themselves?

The situation became bizarre. I was defending the few threads of philosophy that I found meaningful. I was encouraging my students to *be* philosophers, rather than *learn* philosophy. Some succeeded, and that spelled disaster as they refused to adapt to other course demands and requirements. My doubts exploded. But that's another story.

I found myself doubting again in the early 1970s as I undertook a Holy Week fast with a male Methodist minister. I had responded impulsively to a call at a conference. The bombing of Laos and Cambodia was relentless and obscene. "This kind can only be cast out by prayer and fasting." Harry and I signed up. Others withdrew as it became obvious that the action was not sufficient to warrant national publicity. We had two planning sessions: one to work out the arrangements, one for me to meet his wife and children. I'm not sure how I expected my community to respond. We planned to stay in a little inner city church known for its ecumenical openness, to open the doors early and leave them open all day for people to join us, fasting, praying, singing, breaking bread, strategizing local action, etc. There were very mixed reactions: fears for my health, questions of my motivation, concern about the potential "scandal." Against the objections, strengthened by the support of a few understanding friends, I entered wholeheartedly into the week. There were doubts, but I was following something I couldn't name. Going against the tide, taking a clear stand opened me up to new inner resources, stamina, faith, and opened up a world of contacts, new friends. For once I knew I had acted, not logically, but according to my gut and my heart. It was a fairly new experience.

And there have been doubts of a very different sort: relationships that I had come to trust and to rely on, close personal ties that I thought were unbreakable and without shadows. And then the test: Is the way forward theirs or mine? Am I being manipulated? Is this crossroads a time for deeper fidelity or a parting of the ways? How much of myself and my needs can I submerge? Can we work it out or do we give up? There have been different outcomes in different instances, dependent, of course, on the parties involved. Discernment in those emotional moments is almost impossible. Feelings blind us and we are in danger of making drastic and hasty decisions. We could be swallowed up and destroyed in an unhealthy collusion. In these circumstances, doubts are the warning lights cautioning us and moving us to redefine and reassess the truth of the relationship.

PASSAGE THROUGH DOUBT

As I reflect on the more momentous occasions of doubt in my own life, I recognize certain elements common to each experience. There is the moment of standing alone without any evidence, any certitude. Thomas the apostle was an outsider that evening when he returned. He didn't know who was right. He could be isolated further if he refuted the common perceptions of his brothers. He might blow his chance to belong to that inner circle.

Upon his return to Germany from America in 1939, Dietrich Bonhoeffer must have doubted that the course he was taking was the right one. He was associated with those who were intriguing for the downfall of the Hitler regime. Bonhoeffer was abandoning long-held principles of prudence and integrity for a path of closely-woven deceptions and, ultimately, a willingness to murder. They were evils, surely. How great the doubts! He had to face the prospect of complete loss of credibility within his own church, not to mention the bald fact of danger to his own person.

Agnes Mary Mansour must have doubted when she was confronted with the ultimatum of leaving her ministry as Director of the Michigan Department of Social Services or yielding her thirty-year-long membership in her religious order. She must have doubted the Roman Catholic church's expressed commitment to defend the poor. A small portion of the department's budget was allotted to Medicaid funding for abortions. In her position she felt she could not withdraw these resources, which were available to the poor, as long as abortion was legal and she was working for a state institution. She must have doubted the support of her superiors and colleagues in community who did not refuse her resignation from the order. She must have doubted the value of her years of dedication and service within the institutional church, now so seemingly overlooked.

The second element is that of proceeding in the dark, acting in spite of real doubts. Can there be any faithful action without doubts? Aren't we faithful precisely when we move on without the benefit of answers, approvals, guaranteed outcomes? Thomas told it as he felt it: not unless I have something more concrete to go on than your words, your wishful thinking, perhaps. He voiced his doubts and set himself up for the snide judgments and gentle ridicule of succeeding ages.

Dietrich Bonhoeffer was writing *Ethics* at that very crucial time in his life. But theology was useless if it had no praxis, if it provided no wrenching dilemmas. In the winter of 1941-1942 Bonhoeffer told the resistance leaders he was ready to participate in the plot against Hitler.

Agnes Mansour signed the papers of dispensation, making final the separation from her past history and her closest friends. She signed rather than put her community under greater pressure from Rome.

With the act come the consequences. Accepting them, in their entirety, is the third element. The words of a prophet in my own life have often haunted me: "Nonviolence means above all accepting the consequences of your decisions."[1] Thomas's story is collapsed. We do not know what he underwent in the eight days that followed his daring demand. He did not know that there would be another opportunity to claim the risen Jesus.

All is said, in Dietrich Bonhoeffer's story, in his own words: "In helplessness now you see your action is ended; you sigh in relief, your cause committing to stronger hands."[2] On April 5, 1943, he went to prison where he spent the last two years of his life.

Agnes found herself no longer a nun. She had made the impossible choice. She herself was made an example to warn those who dared to disobey institutional authority.

And, in the end, a new truth emerges, whether the journey into doubt be one of life-and-death consequences or more ordinary shifts in attitude and behavior. The fourth element is that new quality of life, that new strength. Hesitation and fear no longer block the way. Truth-in-formation becomes inner truth. Doors open into greater self-knowledge, deeper self-confidence and courage. Thomas's doubts were honored, he was offered a privileged intimacy, and his faith found words, words that would be validated in his missionary vocation, words for which succeeding ages would remember him.

Bonhoeffer whispered to his closest friend, Eberhard Bethge, just before he was led to the scaffold: "This is the end, for me the beginning of life."[3] He had once written of ultimate freedom: "How long we have sought thee in discipline, action and suffering. Dying we now behold thee."[4] He remains a model for resisters and prisoners of conscience, for those who would be a confessing church.

Agnes wrote later of her ministry in Michigan: "We've done many good things, made an impact, had a good platform to speak for the poor and needy. I would do it again."[5] Agnes is but one of many women, in the Roman Catholic church and outside it, who have placed their consciences before political expediency.

The crux of the matter in these bits of biography and in our search for spirituality and faith is that doubts and questions, surfacing from within or pressed upon us from external circumstances, open us up to recognize the truth we are pursuing. Life does not provide advanced answers, a tidy progression of decisions. We discover the meaning of our vocation, of our relationships, of God's place in our lives, through doubts and conflicts and the bits of revelation they give us.

OVERCOMING CERTITUDE

Today we are experiencing a surgence of fundamentalist thinking. Evangelists can be blatant in their claims to the truth. For some, faith is a matter of black and white affirmations. Televangelism, street corner prosyletizing, fundamentalist missionary movements, the public posture of the moral majority—all are expressions of this doubt-free creed. Christianity becomes cheap, a formula, a consumer product. We glimpsed this mentality in the mob calls for the death of Salman Rushdie, in the apparent composure with which Saddam Hussein spoke of a Holy War against the west and the west spoke of the moral rectitude of its cause. During a procession at a recent ecumenical celebration in Liverpool, Bible- and banner-carrying enthusiasts shouted our sin at us, the sin of cooperation (in their minds, betrayal) with "the scarlet woman of Rome."

And not only in the name of religion. Fundamentalism crops its head whenever people become devotees of single issues: political, educational, ethical. Even those who carry feminist banners can become fundamentalists. Or those who flaunt their "greenness." Fundamentalism exists in the avid crusade for anti-abortion, in the non-negotiability of parochial schools, in the massive lobbies for private ownership of weapons, in the patriotic slogan: My country, right or wrong. A fundamentalist mind has no doubts. There is only one way, one right, one truth. The only valid viewpoint is one's own.

As human beings sharing an ever smaller planet-home, as nations whose weapons and methods of warfare are no longer feasible or effective, as neighbors who rely on one another for the most daily of needs, as Christians seeking reconciliation, we are called to be pluralists, students of dialogue, interns in the school of exchange. We must take a position on our own value systems as well as appreciate the value and validity of other world-views. Self-criticism and self-doubts are assets.

I am often puzzled when I meet in ecumenical circles the assumption that Roman Catholics are of one mind. Some people believe that every Roman Catholic shares a common under-standing of the meaning of the Eucharist, that we await the word of the pope or a bishop on such matters as homosexuality or socialism before we form our own consciences. The truth is that among Catholics today, and indeed among members of every denomination, there is a broad spectrum of positions and convic-tions. Some of them match verbalized doctrines of the church and some don't. Some are matters of genuine doubt, of controversy, of radically different points of view. Pluralism is not only healthy, it is essential for mature Christians taking their rightful place in society.

Dialogue is a negative word for some. It is confused with sur-render, with a failure in loyalty. Strength then consists in holding fast to a belief or a set of standards. The truth is that the strong are those who dialogue, who open themselves to the possibility of change and of being influenced. Dialogue requires that we see "the other," politically and religiously, as "equals" and that we take seriously their sincere adherence to their perception of the truth. For many of us, dialogue is too inefficient, too costly. Con-sensus takes time. We are impatient, self-assured, even arrogant in our reliance on fixed doctrine and tradition.

Compromise is taken as a confession of weakness. Instead, it seems to me that our close relationships should teach us that com-promise is necessary for stability and growth. Life and energy are easily blocked without it. There may be some genuine non-negotiables in a situation, certainly in our Christian discipleship, but there are countless instances where differences will only be settled by compromise. Dialogue between churches does not seem to take that into account at times. It is not a matter of one dom-inant party convincing another party to make allowances. It is a matter of openness, mutual flexibility, and costly exchange.

Personal journeys into doubt prepare us to be more open in our human communities. They keep us in touch with our fallibility, our solidarity in the human enterprise of seeking truth. And they point us to the critical task of questioning any captivities and certitudes that our society and our culture attempt to impose on us. Gullibility in absorbing information, regardless of the respectability of the source, is not a virtue. Gullibility has led too often to control, blind obedience, repressed imagination and conscience.

Vulnerability, not gullibility, is a daughter-virtue of doubt. Vulnerability keeps us critiquing and open to criticism, searching and open to being challenged. Vulnerability allows stereotyped values to be turned upside down, to reveal the strength in weakness, the logic of foolishness, the riches in sacrifice. "Masters of human wisdom, people of letters, philosophers, there is no place for you. And the wisdom of this world? God let it fail. At first God spoke the language of wisdom, and the world did not know God in his wisdom. Then God thought of saving the world through the foolishness that we preach" (1 Corinthians 1:20-21).

There is a marvelous image of doubt, of vulnerability, in one of R.S. Thomas's poems. He describes prayer as:

> ...gravel
> flung at the sky's
> window, hoping to attract
> the loved one's attention
> ...peering once
> through my locked fingers
> I thought that I detected
> the movement of a curtain.[6]

It is, after all, faithfulness, not certitude, that is asked of us. "Your faith has saved you." The faithfulness of Thomas who recognized and proclaimed: My Lord and my God. The faithfulness of Dietrich Bonhoeffer who severed his official links with his church when he made his fateful decision. He did not want to make his burden of conscience theirs. The faithfulness of Agnes Mansour whose commitment to ministry to the poor and rejected of society superseded her concern for herself and her security.

"God will bring to light whatever was hidden in darkness and doubt, and will disclose the secret intentions of human hearts" (1 Corinthians 4:5).

THE WORD WAS MADE FLESH

"They were in Bethlehem when the time came for her to have her child, and she gave birth to a son, her firstborn. She wrapped him in clothes and laid him in the manger, because there was no place for them in the living space" (Luke 2:6-7).[1]

Incarnation is like that. It is specific. Jesus was born in that city of that mother. He wore those swaddling clothes and slept in that feeding-trough. It was winter and the inns and private homes were crowded with visitors and census takers. Whatever else is packed into that excerpt, of divinity visiting earth, of rejection and denial of hospitality, it is clearly a statement of the limitations of human existence.

I gaze at children on buses and trains, in strollers on city streets, in doctors' offices and on school playing fields. Each already has a history, a tale of affection and nurturing, or one of neglect and abuse. Each will grow within the limitations of a country, poverty-stricken or affluent, in a family on welfare with one parent or in a comfortable home, amid toys and tantalizing opportunities.

A child in Leeds, England, awaits his father assigned to Northern Ireland. A baby in a hospital in New York fights against AIDS. Children in São Paulo or Delhi live on the streets. A family of five huddles into a tenement flat in east London or a high-rise apartment in Detroit. Other children play happily in nurseries and day care centers while parents work. Nannies replace mothers and fathers, and suburban children are driven to and from school. Different starts in life, but each one limited and situated.

My own childhood was set in a tiny village in rural Wisconsin, amid farmers and laborers. My eight brothers and sisters and I were all raised in the same house. I went to a Roman Catholic parochial elementary school. There were ten in my graduation class. We knew all our neighbors and, because my father ran the local tavern, I knew many people in the township. Few had traveled more than 100 miles from home and fewer still had college degrees or ambitions beyond owning their own farm or business.

As the youngest in the family, I spent a lot of time alone as a child. I became an avid reader from the age of six. Books were scarce and I literally walked door to door begging magazines from the neighbors. Occasionally I had to settle for seed catalogs or farm journals. Libraries existed in another world, a city ten miles away, and I rarely went there. My clothes came by mail-order when I was lucky. I wore hand-me-downs when I wasn't. I walked a portion of the four miles to school in all weathers. With my friends next door, I plucked peonies from a deserted cemetery to carry to church on rogation days. Nieces and nephews were born before I was talking, so there were always children to look after on special occasions and holidays.

It was a small, narrow, limited world of family and seasons and school work and Sunday church. I first tasted "culture" as a day student at a Dominican boarding school, with its historic traditions and wealthy alumnae. It was there that I first saw Renaissance paintings, learned to love the sound of the French language, entered the mysteries of formal etiquette. I began to realize some people were "well off." Luckily, I was a good student and there was equality in the classroom. I may have been in the lowest ranks economically, but I ranked high academically. It was a world rife with books and intoxicating in its opportunities for learning and enlargement.

My first real encounter with fear came late one Saturday in January when I was six. The house filled with smoke and my mother ushered the three of us who were home outside into the frozen night. There had been a spontaneous combustion in our basement and the whole house was threatened. For long months after the near disaster I smelled the charred boards and tasted the sickening smoke. That same year my sister and I were bundled off to live Monday to Friday with a married sister in order to be closer to school. It was an agonizing wrench, weekly good-byes and endurance of loneliness. Even then I took refuge in books and academic achievement. One of my brothers left home in disgrace when I was a toddler and "disappeared" for a decade. World War II was a vague cataclysmic event that swallowed up my other two brothers for several years and grayed my mother's hair. She, the person I most needed in the world, died when I was fifteen. I was desolate, without anchor, crippled in my deepest spirit.

That was the environment in which I lived and moved and had my being for the first eighteen years of my life. When I return there now, it seems so small, so ragged, so deprived a place. Nonetheless, it was there that I learned my first lessons in limitations, in the finiteness of my surroundings, in the necessity of letting go. It was there that my first idols were smashed, my first securities undermined, and I had my first encounters with danger and evil. Priests were not necessarily godly or good. Parents could rent out their children, even if reluctantly. Children could be abused; little girls were especially vulnerable. Sudden global events could disturb and destroy private lives and relationships.

And not only children's lives. Throughout our human existence there are borders and limits: the language we speak, the people who become our friends and associates, the condition of our health, influences of political decisions, local customs, religious upbringing. We live situated lives, wherever we settle, whatever our profession or trade, however determined our resolution to be free agents in control of our destiny.

When I studied philosophy, I was keenly impressed by the existentialist theory that all freedom is situated, that limitations are the givens in our lives. We work within those limits, make choices, decide how and when the restrictions become opportunities for growth. I remember being enthralled by stories of those who overcame their environment, from Abraham Lincoln to Helen Keller, Sojourner Truth, and Elie Wiesel.

A SPIRITUALITY OF THE CONCRETE

Each of us can identify with a teenage suicide, with a young mother brutally raped, with a former colleague now terminally ill with cancer. What if I was in his or her place? What if I faced those limits? What is the story that precedes and follows such tragedies? How important it is that we not lose that sense of solidarity—what it feels like to be depressed, the disappointment of not being chosen for a job, the unexpected death of a spouse, the terror of having a child abducted—because it is that connection with our own creatureliness that forces us to examine anew the meaning of all limitations and losses.

We live in a world of statistics, of mass movements, of instant worldwide communication. We talk about the homeless and the dropouts, the unemployed and the incarcerated, minorities and strangers as if they were studies, generic names, rather than individual human beings with actual histories and concrete dreams and desires. We analyze racial characteristics, we predict proneness to disease, we classify segments of society as we classify books or government secrets. We stamp and label human beings, compile categories of behavior and intelligence quotients. We so easily neglect the stories that lie behind the child abuser, the bag lady, the joy-riding teenager, the contours of family and social life that have helped to create the mercenary or the mentally ill.

We need a spirituality of the concrete that uses personal names, that honors limitations and perceives the hidden gifts buried amid the losses, a spirituality that takes into account our diverse journeys, our social context, our confrontation with the chaos of political tensions and global threats.

I remember the protest marches in the 1970s when we tried to put faces on the Vietnamese and Cambodians who were being bombed and to appeal to those in the military through their own humanity. I remember processions in the 1980s in which we carried placards bearing the names of those who had "disappeared" in Central America. Today we stand in for prisoners of conscience, writing letters on their behalf, keeping their plight visible. The individual faces of Kurdish refugees, of Yugoslavian cousins at war with one another brought close on our TV screens can, if we will, arouse our compassion and our sense of rage.

We tell our own checkered experiences, and the stories of others that we have been privileged to know, to counteract the atmosphere we so prevalently breathe, of abstractions, generalizations, stereotypes, and statistics. It is the personal narrative that anchors us in a deep regard for human life, that enables us to call one another brother and sister, that weaves us together in a single human tapestry. In my story and in yours, we find the ingredients for mutual understanding, for mutual trust, for mutual efforts to find peaceful paths and opportunities for exchange. Our single and collective memories keep our finiteness in focus and teach us to cherish our own humanity.

Our lives are either rooted in values of reverence and respect, in basic patterns of reciprocity and sensitivity, or they flounder amid shifting sands of security and transitory idols. Our limitations either cripple and label us, or we redefine and redeem them. Losses either overwhelm and embitter us, or they dig new channels of openness and compassion in our bruised psyches and spirits.

ROOTEDNESS

Roots are not only historical and biological, they have spiritual dimensions. I grew up amid pastures and swollen creeks. My childhood games had them as background. I had a favorite apple tree, which was my refuge when duty called and my sanctuary when I had a new book. I loved the seasons, feared storms, washed my hair in rain water, picked fruit from local trees and vines. I rode a bicycle on country lanes, tramped and sleighed in the snow. The largest building I knew was the parish church. I was deprived, you might say, of travel and luxuries. But equally limited are the children who grow up in polluted city air, amid cement sidewalks and relentless traffic, who don't taste fresh vegetables, smell garden flowers, walk barefoot, or understand the connection between rippling wheat fields and cellophane-wrapped loaves.

The challenge in many lives today is to find some roots in nature. We are beginning to learn the importance of partnership with creation. We are beginning to see that neglect of that relationship underlies many of our national and global problems: acid rain, contaminated food chains, the greenhouse effect, periodic flooding. We are at last turning for counsel to those whose roots in nature are centuries deep and for whom creation is the first teacher: the Native Americans, the aboriginals, the people of the land. "This we know. The earth does not belong to us. We belong to the earth. This we know. All things are connected like the blood which unites one family."[2] "God loves everything you love, and a mess of stuff you don't. But more than anything else, God loves admiration. I think it pisses God off if you walk by the color purple in a field somewhere and don't notice it."[3] "In order to love each other, we have to love the garden. In order to love the garden, we have to love each other."[4]

Within the limitations of western urban life, of isolated suburban neighborhoods, of mobile and anonymous existence, how do we restore a rootedness in nature? How do we redeem the images that haunt us of Hiroshima, Three Mile Island, Chernobyl, Bhopal, repeated oil spills? We start by placing ourselves on the side of those who protect rain forests, save dying species, defend the rights of the homeless and the landless, by consciously and sparingly using resources, questioning and limiting our consumption, enjoying our park lands and countrysides. However slow we may have been to hearken to nature's wisdom, we can still commit ourselves to a healthier environment, a more equitable distribution of food, a renewed respect for all that lives and grows and beautifies our lives.

The Wisconsin community in which I had roots as a child included my family, extended and large, the village of Louisburg, and the parish of St. Joseph's. It was a small community by comparison to today's national and international networks and organizations. But I learned the importance of looking out for those in need, pulling together in crisis, protecting the defenseless, and exchanging griefs and joys.

Today's rootless society advocates a ruthless pursuit of self-fulfillment, of individual well-being, with comforts ensured and future guaranteed. Responsibilities and concern more or less end with one's family and one's well-earned, well-deserved private accomplishments. Education, career, possessions are the most important goals in life. Challenges to that point of view are quickly labeled romantic, socialist, revolutionist. Yet, Vincent Donovan says of the United States that its greatest need is to find a sense of community again. "Americans are among the loneliest people in the world...They lock themselves in their homes as protections for themselves and their possessions. They buy terrible weapons of destruction to defend themselves. They refuse to become involved in the desperate needs of their neighbors or to depend in any way on their neighbors for their own needs."[5]

The true test of our rootedness in community, it would seem, is our sensitivity to those whose lives have been unstable and insecure: those in foster homes, institutions, exile, refugee camps. A second test is our openness to balancing and reconciling our primary commitments and personal responsibilities with those we have to our global village and our planetary community.

I hardly knew Protestants existed until I was a young adult. My roots in faith were Roman Catholic through and through. I studied the catechism far more than the Bible. The effects of sin were deeply imprinted on my young conscience. The lives of the saints, rosaries, novenas, incense and bells, Sunday Mass, and frequent confession were familiar ingredients of faith. It was limited and narrow. But I did experience family worship, both at home and in church. I learned that faith informed human events: from crop failures to bankruptcies, from marriage promises to funeral farewells. The cloud of witnesses, those who had been faithful, in history and in real life, were my heroes and heroines.

The search today for roots in faith ranges from pilgrimages to India to youth camps in Assisi. There are multiple explanations for lukewarm faith, sporadic religious practice, disregard of tradition, rejection of communal worship. Some formerly faithful are substituting recreation or health pursuits or athletics for spiritual exercises. Others turn to the occult or to new age philosophies or to therapies. Some give up altogether on religion of any ilk: Just as satisfying to wash one's car as dress for church, more satisfying to join Greenpeace or Friends of the Earth than to support the latest maintenance project of the local parish. A recent article attempts to get at it: "Perhaps the church mistrusts God's people. It seems afraid to encourage them to enjoy the world...My experience is that if people feel loved, trusted, and valued, they blossom in all sorts of generous ways. The church rather stunts our growth."[6]

In a new book on spiritual growth in children, Robert Coles says that the rituals and rules of formal religious experience can harm children's spirituality and can deaden their youthful energies.[7] Another attempt to analyze the apathy and drift away from formal churchgoing acknowledges that the churches as we know them may well be dying. "The degree to which they are social and historical constructions is greater than we usually realize...Nevertheless, the Christian tradition is by no means bankrupt. It is still the means by which and the context in which many people in the Western world will pursue their quest for meaning, for what is worth being committed to, for God."[8]

Some of our religious roots are badly in need of transplanting and uprooting. But we can't find our way without some existential knowledge of where we've come from or where we belong. The paradox of roots is that they limit us, but they also give us a home and a sense of direction. "I am the vine and you are the branches. As long as you remain in me and I in you, you bear much fruit. But apart from me you can do nothing" (John 15:5). One of our tasks today is to help find roots, deeply human roots, for those who wander homeless in a spiritual desert.

WHO DEFINES LIMITS?

A second discovery we make when we face the limitations that life imposes on us is the relativity of limits themselves. So many terms we use, presumably with definite meanings, are not univocal. "Deprivation" for some may be "opportunity" for others. Would I have had such a yearning to learn if I had not been deprived of books as a child? What qualifies us to judge whether or not a nation is developed or undeveloped, a people civilized or uncivilized? Whether families are backward or culturally different? What constitutes success or achievement? Who are the handicapped in our world?

Security, too, has many false faces. We talk so glibly of national security as if it were something unarguable. Yet all the arms and defenses in the world do not make our city streets secure or our economic systems reliable. The limitations to our security are apparent in the drugs that are available, the unemployment figures, the fear that prevents even the well-intentioned from opening their doors or hearts to strangers.

We talk about possessions. But what do we really possess? Our homes, subject to threats from intruders or mortgage institutions? Our TVs and stereos and VCRs, so easily worn out or surpassed by new, better, models? Our cars and recreational vehicles, so vulnerable? Our jewels and expensive toys, which we guard so zealously and which we fear to exhibit or use?

We all shun the experience of pain. The acme of human ingenuity is a pain-free existence, hence easy access to medications of all descriptions, to jacuzzis and electrical appliances for every need and whim: something to make us tan that won't burn us, something to make us youthful but not damage our skin, something to add to our luxury and comfort but not to make us obese. The range of our search for this painless state extends from cosmetic surgery to cordless phones, remote TV controls, and an infinite variety of diet foods. Yet what adds to the joy of childbirth but the pain of waiting and even of labor? What increases the joy of every reunion but the pain of separation? What are feasts without fasts and music without silence? What is love without sacrifice and gift of self? Is not the Prophet correct: "The deeper that sorrow carves into your being, the more joy you can contain. Is not the cup that holds your wine the very cup that was burned in the potter's oven? And is not the lute that soothes your spirit the very wood that was hollowed with knives?"[9]

The issue is not one of limitations. Our security and our successes are limited, as are our enjoyment of things and our experience of happiness. The issue is one of discernment. What do we really value, with its built-in limitations? What mattered most to us as we moved from childhood to adulthood? What are our greatest treasures in life? Is life for us a process of growth in wisdom rather than an endless series of accumulations and rewards? Is life itself a limited experience, opening onto something which eye has not seen, nor mind can imagine? "We know that the whole creation groans and suffers the pangs of birth. Not creation alone, but even ourselves...we groan in our innermost being, eagerly awaiting the day when God will adopt us" (Romans 8:22-23), when the limitations of life become the glorious identification by which we are recognized as God's sons and daughters, when our scars are honored as achievements, when healing what is broken is as significant a service as manufacturing new items of comfort.

Life is limited. No relationship is perfect. The world we know is finite. Parents are fallible, as are all authority figures. All our heroes and heroines have their moments and their seasons. Joys pass, all too quickly. No trial lasts forever. Idolatry, a friend often quotes to me, is thinking the whole sea exists in a cockleshell. Coming to terms with our idolatries is one of life's most difficult lessons. "Along the whole length of the road, there are numberless tiny deaths...We let something slip from our hands in order to be free to grasp a new and greater gift. We die in order to live more fully, over and over again. And if during the years that are given us in this life we can form an instinctive habit of death and resurrection, then when the final, unavoidable letting-go is demanded of us, we shall be able to accept it quite naturally with sure and certain hope: Welcome, life."[10]

God wastes nothing. God is the memory that forgets no one. God does not think or act in terms of limits, but rather potential, the talent to be turned into more talents. That is why Micah said: Only one thing is asked of you, that you act justly, love tenderly, and walk humbly with your God. That is why Solomon was affirmed in his request, not for long years of governance or victory over enemies, but for the gift of discernment. That is why Joseph is succinctly called "just" and Mary "blessed." Openness, the capacity for wisdom, is more precious than all the virtues and the one lifelong companion we need. There are but two commandments: to love God with an undivided heart and to love your neighbor as you would be loved yourself.

> God sits weaving
> She gathers
> the rags of hard work
> initiatives for peace
> protests against injustice
> all the seemingly little and weak
> words and deeds offered sacrificially
> She is weaving them all
> into a new tapestry."[11]

REDEEMING LOSSES

We have all experienced displacement of one sort or another: being sent to boarding school, travel to or life among a different culture, the experience of being a minority, loss of position or status, rejection or betrayal by a friend, loss of loved ones, amputations, and so on.

I recently had a letter from a revered elderly friend. She could only speak of losses. They are the hallmark of her present experience: her own health, a dying community of family and friends, the pain of accompanying younger relatives through sickness and diminishment, the necessity of laying down beloved and familiar tasks and entrusting duties to others. Nonetheless her openness to life and its wisdom shines through.

I remember clearly the first time I appeared in public after my mastectomy. It didn't matter that it was unnoticeable to others. I felt the amputation and felt as well a new identification with all the deformed, maimed, disfigured persons in our world. I didn't choose that crossing-over. It happened because of my loss.

For that is what loss offers, a crossing-over. Not painless or uncostly, but as part of the process of becoming more fully human. We cross over to solidarity with a wider group of people, to a wider perspective from which to judge what has been left behind, to a new experience of creatureliness, or of presence, or of vulnerability. If we do not thwart it, loss opens us to new knowledge of ourselves and of others who have lost and lived and learned.

We recently spent a day reflecting with the members of the Mission Department of the United Reformed Church. For a couple of hours we shared personal moments that we felt had shaped or influenced our understanding of mission. I was moved as person after person related an experience of crossing-over: to a different culture, a different style of worship or celebration, a "foreign" world. New questions surfaced as they made the cross-over: questions about their own culture, their own manner of praying, their own church. They now had new criteria for looking at their habitual patterns and valued traditions.

We cannot minimize loss. It is stark, cruel, and often final. We certainly cannot speak for those whose loss has broken hearts, or families, or hope. We cannot assume resurrection, in our own lives or for those who face pain and death, whatever its guise. But loss need not always be all loss. Even displacements bring gifts in their train if we do not refuse them, if we are not subject to idolatry, if we are alert to life's paradoxes, if we can trust the dynamic of life itself to carry us forward into deeper places of connection. "Have I not told you that if you believe, you will see the glory of God?" (John 11:40). "There is hope for a tree: if cut down, it will sprout again, its new shoots will keep on coming" (Job 14:7). "The one who cares only for his [her] own life will lose it; the one who loses his [her] life for my sake will find it" (Matthew 10:39).

Limitations are the material out of which we choose and carve the unique paths that constitute our journey into God. "When you pass through the waters, I will be with you...When you walk through the fire, you will not be burned...Look, I am doing a new thing, I am opening up a way in the wilderness" (Isaiah 43:2,19). Losses are the openings that force us—painfully, it is true—into new stages of maturity and of faith. "I know what my plans are for you, plans to save you and not to harm you, plans to give you a future, and to give you hope" (Jeremiah 29:11).

This chapter began with the account of Jesus' birth into poverty, into a hostile world. Jesus ended his brief controversial life on a hill outside Jerusalem. "They nailed him onto the cross and divided his clothes among themselves, casting lots to decide what each should take" (Mark 15:24). His companions in death were two thieves. Shades of his beginning: an unfriendly world, the company of outcasts, nakedness, rejection. Limitations and loss.

"What we are witnessing," writes J.V. Taylor, "as we stand before the crucified Christ is not a death but life—life so vividly and intensely alive that it meets death and goes down into nothingness and contains both death and annihilation."[12] The one who has truly lived, in spite of constraining limitations and agonizing losses, is free to die. The limitations and losses that mar and mark all our lives shape our identities. Those identities can never be lost. They can only blossom into greater integrity and deeper wisdom. Into life's hands we commend our spirits.

CHAPTER SIX

WILL YOU ALSO LEAVE ME?

"The hour is coming; indeed it has come, when you will be scattered each one to your home, and you will leave me alone" (John 16:32).

I have often wondered why John is the only one of the four evangelists who does not relate the episode of Jesus' struggle in the Garden of Olives. His narrative moves directly from the prayer of Jesus in the supper room to Judas's betrayal. Was it too painful for him to try to put into words, especially since he had been one of the three chosen to watch and pray with Jesus at the ominous hour? Since he too had fallen asleep and failed to give Jesus the companionship and comfort he might have offered? Was it because he had missed "the hour" that Jesus had predicted so many times, and he had not quite been able to forgive himself? Perhaps, and I suppose we'll never know, it is why John devotes so much emphasis to the farewell words of Jesus at the Last Supper. He had heard those and they contain all the hints of the anguish and fear that Jesus must have felt later that night, alone in the garden. "If the world hates you, remember that the world hated me before you." "If they persecuted me, they will persecute you too." "The hour is coming when anyone who kills you will claim to be serving God." In John's rendition, it is all said in Jesus' statement: "You will leave me alone."

Recently, a friend whose husband had died just weeks previously said to me: "What do people do who don't have faith?" When our pain is at its most extreme we Christians turn toward the Garden of Olives. We contemplate the suffering, the acute loneliness of Jesus, and we find strength to take up the weighty cross that is ours and ours alone. No other incident in Scripture, in the whole of our tradition, quite speaks to the depths of our ache as does that nocturnal scene. That is what it is like, we instinctively confirm—agony, bloody sweat, a soul sorrowful enough to die.

Two days after Christmas this year a mother walked with her two daughters, six and eight, along a path bordering on a canal. She was carrying her seven-month-old son. Her husband was fishing further away. There was an accident. The two girls slipped into the canal, perhaps playing, perhaps not paying full attention. The mother panicked. She reached into the water to try to help them and lost her balance. The baby slipped out of her arms and both tumbled into waters fifteen feet deep. Only the mother survived, aided by fishermen. The tragedy haunted all who heard of it. Who can understand her pain, and the father's? How will the agony ever pass? They are alone in their grief, their total loss of family, of life and of laughter.

NUMBNESS AND EXILE

My own life has produced two periods of extreme isolation and loneliness. I say "periods" deliberately because they were not discrete events of which I could say: It happened that day in that year at that hour and it ended at that precise time. The first was my mother's prolonged illness and death, which cut short my adolescence (I was fifteen when she died) and catapulted me into premature adulthood. The second was my own "breakdown," which put an abrupt close to my career as professor of philosophy and exiled me to a three-year stretch of inner meaninglessness and outer isolation (I was thirty-one years old). The link between the two experiences is a deep sense of loneliness. The difference between the two is that I was acutely aware of what was happening to me in the latter, and completely baffled by the changes that the former were making in my spirit.

I was depressed when my mother died. Perhaps I had been depressed at times during her long invalidism from severe strokes. I missed so terribly the special relationship I had had as the youngest of nine children. I ached to tell her my school tales and share my dreams as I had always done, but she was no longer able to speak to me. I mourned the loss of the spontaneous teasing and the reliable companionship that were part and parcel of my life. I was angry that God took my mother whom I needed and left me with my father with whom there had always been distance and reserve. I was so unready to make my own decisions, to move out of that carefully constructed milieu of my mother's love and counsel. Most of all, I did not understand my own depression, loss of interest, resignation to endless days of coping without hope of her presence and protection. I didn't even know how to allow others to help me. Life went on, though everything about it was different. I shut down parts of myself, adapted to new patterns of living, and grew up without ado.

The most remote thought in my mind when I was thirty was the possibility of finding myself incarcerated in a mental hospital, deprived even of the necklace-cross that was part of my religious habit (I might use it as a weapon against myself), an object of pity and grave concern to family and community. My Ph.D. was still fresh in my possession. My students were avid and devoted. My life extended before me, a career in teaching, partnership with colleagues who had once taught me. How could I know that God was about to "break in" precisely where I felt strong and invulnerable, my mental and emotional stability? And that is what happened. Whether it was through strain and concentration, long months of loss of sleep, or the accumulation of grief and anger over years (possibly since my fifteenth year), I woke up one day unable to focus, to function, to find my way to my classes.

It was the onset of a mysterious numbness that crept into my whole being, caused me to want to die, closed down all my connections with the basic ingredients of life: color, activity, conversation, relationships. I could not feel the wind on my face, the hand that clasped mine, my sister's death from cancer, the ground under my feet, the meaning of anything I heard or read. I was alone in my deep dark tunnel and there was no end to it, it seemed. I simply sat there—mute, pitiable, wasted. But even worse, I was monitoring what was happening to me. My emotions had shut down, but not my mind. I knew others were worried that I might be suicidal. I knew that the medical staff was observing my reactions. I knew my family was grieving. I knew I wasn't going to do what mental patients did: play silly games, cut out felt squares, do paint-by-number. I knew that I wanted to be whole and human again, in touch with my students, belonging somewhere.

I remember one aimless walk when I was released from the hospital. It was evening and lights were coming on in the houses I passed. With great envy, I glimpsed normal life, the supper table, children, noise, and clutter. I was outside normal life. I remember my keen sense of suspension: no job, no home, no future. I longed to have roots again. I moved around a lot in that period, but fit in nowhere. Time was a massive burden. Nothing I did seemed important. Only a few gained entry in any sense to the darkness and the loneliness I kept inside. Outwardly, I looked and acted like a well person, a little withdrawn perhaps, but no hysteria, few demands on others. I just waited and waited and waited for life to return. And, with prodding and support from a psychotherapist become friend, it did. Slowly, in tiny gasps and wisps, till one day I knew I had emerged from my tomb. My senses were alive. My concentration had returned. I was interested in people and events. I looked forward once again to a new day.

One of the particular outcomes of that experience of depression is a sense of solidarity that I feel so readily with others who are isolated. I spoke of my depression two years ago in a presentation to a large crowd of people. I was not surprised later when a man sought me out and wanted to share his own burden. He was deeply depressed, and laden with guilt as well because of the pain it caused his wife and children. In his description of his malaise and anxiety, I experienced again those numbing feelings: lack of energy, immense efforts to "perform," the dull grayness of all life's details. I met this same man recently. He is still clinically depressed. He looks worn and drawn, his marriage is faltering, he has further guilt. How long, O God, will you be angry? How much can one human being sustain? And how helpless we are to reach out across the chasm that is loneliness and despair!

I watched a TV program on one of the French hostages liberated after three years in captivity in Lebanon. He was a different person after his release, with completely different priorities and sensitivities. I understood some of his inability to cope and his need for solitude and protection from people. I have a sense of identity and kinship with people in prisons and in mental institutions. Their situations remind me of forming experiences of my own that I do not want to forget. Similarly, I ache with those who have said final farewells to loved ones and who try to endure the absence and the loneliness that floods in. I appreciate the effort they must make to re-build, to find new modes of intimacy with that beloved person. The time it takes, the tears, the emptiness, the inexpressible grief. The best word I can find to sum up those experiences is exile, exile from normal life, exile from expected modes of behavior, from the comfortable familiarity of life as it was before the pain set in.

There are a number of options that one can choose or fall into during those agonizing periods. We don't always turn automatically or effectively to the Christ of Gethsemane and find courage and endurance. Some people, at least for a time, need a narcotic, be it sleep or frenetic activity, the distraction of a remote sojourn, or the help of medication. Some of us try to deny the pain, to repress it, to pretend, to lock up the anger or the grief and to withhold ourselves from others. Others struggle openly, protesting, projecting, even destroying. If we are fortunate, we will at some point enter the pain, dwell in it, even wallow in it, so that its truth reaches us, wounds us however severely, purges us in some strange way of the element of isolation and of a personal monopoly on human anguish. Only then can the experience open us to its universal implications: our common humanity, the gifts of vulnerability and solidarity and compassion, the potential of human courage, and, yes, of personal suffering. "All human hearts dwell in the same loneliness. If I follow the longing in that loneliness, the longing for relatedness, I can hope that it will take me not only to God but also to the heart of humankind."[1]

Am I saying that the pain of loneliness can be redeemed? Yes, redeemed and possibly transformed. We have only to consider the witness of numerous contemporaries to affirm that this can be true. What benefits have been born from Nelson Mandela's isolation and imprisonment? From the bravery and boldness of Vaclav Havel's pursuit of truth into and through the prison camps of Czechoslovakia? From the courage of Central American men and women who have escaped tyranny and gone into hiding? The blood of martyrs is the seed of a renewed church, a reality repeated again and again in the deaths and resurrections that have occurred in El Salvador and Guatemala and Honduras. While freedom and hope are still in labor in many parts of the world, signs appear everywhere of the persistence of truth and generous sacrificial love—sometimes an individual offering, sometimes the witness of a community or a committed group of disciples, sometimes the slow conversion of a hitherto impregnable system.

In our individual lives, you and I have seen the new energies that arise from the ashes of burnt-out hopes and dreams. We watch families in Northern Ireland, victims of tragedies, parents of abducted or slain children. We watch our sisters bury their husbands and bravely pick up their lives. We watch our friends accompany others through death from cancer or AIDS and then preserve the beauty and integrity of that snuffed-out life. We watch mothers and fathers embracing the diminished but radiant life of a brain-damaged child. We watch the elderly who bear their ills graciously, the poor who celebrate their survival, the sinned-against who forgive the sinner, and, yes, the depressed who cling to the one small thread of mere physical existence.

LESSONS OF SURVIVAL

Specific lessons and insights result from loneliness entered into and transformed. One of the most painful aspects of my depression was the experience of *reduction* that had a number of expressions. First of all, life was reduced to a matter of elemental but quite insurmountable tasks: washing my face, moving from room to room, deciding how to spend the hours of the day. No real accomplishments, nothing useful to show, no memorable thoughts. Days were all the same, dull gray and monotonously routine. Instead of being in command of my destiny, I was reduced to an object of scrutiny, of concern, dependent upon others who decided my treatment, my place of abode, whether I was progressing or regressing. Perhaps the loneliest dimension was the loss of my own image, my reduced identity. I had been intelligent, respected, admired, loved. I had been a leader, a faithful friend, a responsible member of a community. I had gifts to share, I was needed. I made a difference. Now I was a patient, sick. Some were afraid of me. I was useless. I felt unwanted, a burden. I could only receive, beg, join the ranks of the undesirables and the forgotten. It was a stripping. I lost what I treasured. I was reduced to poverty and to a childish dependency. Henceforth life would be unexpected, undeserved, a gift. Losses henceforth should be experienced with new insight: Nothing is mine, all can disappear. What is the firm foundation upon which I base my life?

A second lesson I learned is the gratuitousness of life itself, of energy, of natural beauty, mystery, simple daily comforts, and delight. They cannot be taken for granted. They can be so overshadowed that life becomes a heavy plodding through indistinct, lack-luster, eternally long moments. I spent three months during that long exile with my sister and her family. There was a three-year-old in the house. She alone did not see me as sick; that in itself gave me a spark of life. We would go outdoors together, to walk, to play in the leaves, to toss balls. I was fascinated by her spontaneity (I had none), her joy in the flinging of colored leaves (I could barely lift an arm to throw them), her delight in having a playmate (who could possibly want my company?). She was a therapist for me. It took a long time before I could appreciate for myself the taste of good food, the texture of laundered towels or of the grass under bare feet, before I could enjoy gardens and games, visitors and books, ventures into shopping malls and homes of friends, before I could actually rely on the returned energy and sense of well-being. For so long I was afraid it would evaporate again and leave me numb and lost. Better it not return at all than to undergo its fading a second time. What is that mysterious force called energy or spirit that makes life meaningful, attractive, purposeful? I do not want to lose the mystery, the thrill, of that force.

My own psychic wilderness taught me that the desert is an important experience in our lives, that life is not all success, movement, entertainment, excitement. The deep gulfs that enveloped me left me with a need for solitude and space. It left a residue, a desire for distance, in order to make interaction and relationship more whole. I can sometimes now be more lonely in a crowd than when I am secluded. The desert sustains something in us, be it an opportunity to question life's meaning, a perspective, a time for recovering and healing. Perhaps there is a wilderness need in each of us and we don't actually come to know it until we enter our own real wilderness. Even today when I set foot in a vast expanse, a forest, a moor, a far-reaching countryside, I feel a release inside me. I belong here, where I am but a speck on a huge map, where there is everything yet to discover, where there is room to breathe and to locate oneself anew on life's landscape.

There is a survival lesson in confronting the darkness within. It makes it more likely that we can face some of the darkness without. We learn something about confidence amid threats, security amid ambiguity. Jesus made the desert experience a prerequisite for the launching of a mission. There is a tradition in the Scriptures of lonely treks through the wilderness in search of new ways to live.

On the other hand, too much isolation diminishes our humanity. We need community to know and to grow. We have our identity through others. They give us our place, our role, our reason to be. Community connects us to a larger world. Jon Sobrino was absent from the university in San Salvador the night the six Jesuits and the two women workers were killed. He said later that when he returned to what had been their common home he felt lost inside, that what had connected him to his daily life had been severed. His companions and colleagues were the channels by which and through which he saw and felt his surroundings. We filter our experiences through those who live and work with us. Their meaning is influenced and shaped by others' perceptions and responses. Loneliness is a call to return to community, where we are known, where our vulnerability is honored and protected.

Loneliness forces us to be in touch with both the poverty and the potential of our lives. It forces us to take responsibility for our destiny. It reminds us that before God we are weak and incomplete. In the words of a poet-friend:

> I like people who leak,
> who carry Elmer's glue
> in little bottles
> in inside coat pockets, just in case
> I like broken whole ones
> who need not
> windowdress, prove themselves,
> paint S's on their chests
> nor pretend their limits away
> ...I like people
>
> who have some room left.[2]

Finally, loneliness points us to God. So often when we find ourselves in an emotional state of conflict, worry, or personal injury, we turn spontaneously and hungrily to prayer. In our woundedness and dependency, God becomes accessible. We are in illustrious company. Job did the same: "I know that my redeemer lives...with my own eyes I will see him. How my heart rejoices" (Job 19:25-26). And Jeremiah: "Yahweh, you test the just and probe the heart and mind" (Jeremiah 20:12). And the psalmist: "See if my steps have gone astray, and lead me in your eternal way" (Psalm 139:24). And Peter: "Lord, save me'" (Matthew 14:30). And the multitude of half-whole, partially complete, inadequately human, wounded healers of the gospels: the blind and the lame, the leper and the tax collector, the pharisee and the prostitute, the centurion and the thief. Lord, if you want, you can make me clean. Jesus, son of David, have mercy on me. Lord, remember me when you come into your kingdom.

"The anguish and terror of the loneliness appear again and again, taking ever new forms. Each time our solitary self meets them, we have to come to terms anew with the deficiency, the lack we experience in the loneliness...Each time we have to see what the loneliness had to do with God and what we must do to make the anguish and terror give way to love. Each time we have to pass from a sense that God is transcendent in Kant's meaning of the term, beyond human experience, to a sense that God is immanent, that our experience is from and of and toward God."[3]

The hour will come, if not before, then at the hour of our death, when we, too, will be left alone. If the lonely moments and lonely spans of our lives have taught us to welcome and sift wisdom from that hour, an angel from heaven will surely come to us, too, and minister to us. "Be not afraid. I am with you always until the end of the world" (Matthew 28:20).

CHAPTER SEVEN

A CHARCOAL FIRE, FISH, AND BREAD

"When they landed, they saw a charcoal fire there with fish on it and some bread...Jesus said to them: 'Come and have breakfast'" (Luke 21:9, 12).

On Fridays my mother smelled of fish. For all the years of my childhood, she fried fish on Fridays for literally hundreds of people. In the summer, sweat ran down her neck as she stood over the hot stove, four large frying pans sizzling away. In the winter, the kitchen was full of steam while she wiped her greasy hands on an old towel and churned out plate after plate of freshly fried perch or haddock, two slices of brown bread, and a large dill pickle. Even though it was part of the business trade she shared with my father, she cooked that fish as if it were for members of her own family. After all, her customers were family. My mother's vocation was to feed others.

My family has always gathered around food, so much so that it is the kitchen that stands out in my memories of family events. Even today family reunions are largely kitchen-centered, with one of my sisters as chief hostess and chef. Often the children are fed first, then the adults, nieces, nephews, uncles, friends. All are welcome to the bounty and the banter.

Meals have been sacred occasions all my life. As a child I was never sure who would join us at the evening meal: neighbors, strangers, elderly visitors, boarders, even sales people or repair persons. There were wedding buffets, church picnics, funeral dinners, birthday celebrations, harvest suppers, festive meals on holidays, and the regular Sunday spread. I might return from school to the inviting smell of bread baking, the tantalizing aroma of simmering soup, drifts of spice and pickle during a canning season. One of my first awarenesses of the convent as home, as a belonging place, was the familiar smell of fresh bread wafting through the corridors as I came in from outdoors.

It is a tradition that many of us in this age are attempting to recapture: the centrality of a community meal, the sacredness of growing and sharing food, the mystery of bread-breaking and of table fellowship.

For most of us food is an assumed commodity, available on demand and in a wide variety of choices. Food is one of the symbols of the changes that have gripped our generation, a change with implications far beyond diet and lifestyle. It has affected the way we relate to one another, our understanding and experience of hospitality. It has affected our value system as consumers and producers of food, and raised questions about justice and basic human rights. It has had its repercussions on our religious faith, our rituals, and our sacraments.

Like so many other things in our efficiency-minded society, food is something we instantly produce. Fast-food restaurants, machines dispensing cardboard-wrapped pastries and sundries, packaged frozen food for fast consumption, microwave miracles. Supermarket displays, in their variety and awesome abundance, are breathtaking even to First World purchasers. The gap grows between the manner and means of growing food and the cellophane-bound products we select from the shelves.

Our generation has time for eating, but less interest in common meals. We often eat on the run, we "pick up" our food, we eat while we do other things (hold meetings, watch TV), we stand at "stalls" in railway stations and airports. Food is available almost everywhere, consumed almost everywhere, and litter bins bulge with the plastic and paper remains. Families are caught in the dilemma of finding one evening a week when all can be together. Family reunions occur less and less frequently as members move, necessarily and freely, from one part of the country or world to another. The truth is that we often do not have time or energy to be hospitable to those with whom we live. Especially in the United States, we have become a hamburger, coke, ice cream cone culture. Or, from another point of view, we have produced a class of people who eat from garbage cans or survive on dog food, stale bread, and the occasional handout.

Lifestyles that prevent families and communities from sharing common meals prevent so much more. Meals are events. The place and time and circumstances are as important as the food—times of intimacy and of in-depth discourse, bonds of love and friendship renewed and reinforced. My deepest friendships have been nurtured and honored through repeated occasions of bread-breaking: at a local restaurant, in our own dining rooms, at picnics, or at the communion table. My experience has taught me that eating with someone from whom I am estranged causes either indigestion or conversion. Sharing food is too intimate an act to leave us untouched. We sense the sacramentality of food at unexpected moments: as we pass a bakery, accept a child's offer of a crookedly-cut cookie, witness the first bite of a wedding cake, embrace one another with our eyes across a broken dinner roll.

Our contemporary concern for health has awakened some of us to examine our eating habits. Our interest in the environment has produced some critique of our abuse of resources. But it will take a lot of reflection and conversion before we perceive food as a gift of creation and meals as sacred moments of hospitality and sharing.

SPONTANEOUS HOSPITALITY

Even a cursory reading of the gospels highlights the importance of meals in the community life of Jesus' disciples. We have glimpses that bread-breaking and table fellowship were an integral part of the formation they received. And that the experience of sharing food was profoundly connected with the gift of hospitality and with a recognition of God's presence among them.

Having never taken up fishing, it is difficult for me to imagine the exhaustion and frustration the disciples were feeling after a long night of laying nets without any catch. Impossible then to fully appreciate their amazement and joy when their net was almost instantly full of fish. There was a double miracle. Undoubtedly Simon Peter, Thomas, Nathaniel, and some of the others had returned to their fishing occupation after Jesus' death. Suddenly they were surprised by Jesus' presence. Peter was quick to identify him, but the eyes of the others were opened when they saw the charcoal fire, with fish frying and some bread. "They knew it was the Lord."

Breakfast by the lake of Tiberias was a spontaneous occasion of hospitality. Young people at a recent gathering, reflecting on community and a sense of belonging, were asked about marks of a Christian community. One of the marks most affirmed was "spontaneous hospitality." I realized afresh how significant spontaneity was to this group of young people. In my middle-class, middle-aged mentality, hospitality is a real value, but I prefer it to be planned, structured, within certain limits, and under certain controls. These youths were saying "spontaneous" hospitality, precisely that which is open-ended, unannounced, unplanned, unlimited, unqualified.

This kind of hospitality is associated perhaps with the people of Latin America or Africa, with their inimitable invitation to share whatever is available: a glass of water, a plate of beans, a banquet of enchiladas or casssava. Or with India. I remember being invited to the home of some local Christians. Three of us were guests of honor, and three places were set at the table. Much to my embarrassment, the entire family stood around the table while we ate, pleased that we were enjoying their food, content to serve and to entertain us.

I find resonance in the parable of the banquet and the incident at Simon's house. It was not those for whom the banquet was planned who appreciated the feast, but those who responded spontaneously to the invitation at the last minute, without notice: the poor, the crippled, and the blind. It was not his host whom Jesus found hospitable, in spite of the lavishness of his menu. It was the uninvited one Jesus praised, the one who spontaneously washed Jesus' feet and wasted precious perfume. Similarly, at

Levi's feast, Jesus was at odds with those who condemned the company he kept, not with those "tax collectors and sinners" who shared the food and fellowship.

Is it not relevant that Jesus' first miraculous sign was performed at a wedding feast? It was traditional to extend the festivities with the drinking of wine, hence the significance of "saving the best wine till last" when many guests would no longer be able to discern quality. Was the gathering of the 5000 on the hillside not an appropriate occasion to make a lasting impression on a large crowd? Jesus gratefully accepted the bread and fish offered, distributed them, then even had the leftovers collected—a moment of revelation, of miraculous sharing, of modeling the mystery of generosity and exchange. Who could mistake the meaning of Jesus' words about the sheep and the goats and qualifications for entering God's new community? Did you feed the hungry? Did you offer a cup of cold water to the one who asked? Did you share life with those in need?

I have seen the miracle of the loaves and fishes re-enacted night after night in an inner city hall. No matter how long the line, no matter how nervous the servers become, the food stretches, more is found, and all are fed. People from vastly different backgrounds meet, their worlds connect, however briefly, and all are humanized and liberated by the sacred event of the meal.

I have seen the story of the magic soup re-lived in countless forms. A risk-taker offers a magic nail or stone to make soup for a suspicious village. Their curiosity slowly draws them into making it a cooperative community venture. Reluctant landowners and shopkeepers contribute leftover vegetables or "seconds" in produce. Those who have more are prompted to share with those who have less. Christian Aid, Bread for the World, Oxfam, Operation Breadbasket: All are catalysts to release the compassionate instincts latent in the secure and comfortable. In the delivery and distribution of food people in distant places become real, and those who give hospitality also become real in the process of exchange.

I have seen the transformation in ordinary places like trains and hospital waiting rooms, when a sandwich is produced and offered, or a candy bar is broken in half. Words are not necessary. The exchange of food suffices. Barriers are dropped, fear fades in that space of a sacred moment.

Those of us who work ecumenically believe that transformation could come from greater hospitality at our altar-tables. More and more laity are questioning the priority of church discipline over Christian discipleship. It is less and less possible for many to hear the theological arguments in the face of their experience of friendship and shared faith. I find it hard to believe that God is as custodial and discriminating in the gift of Jesus Christ as some of our churches profess. What was the meaning of Jesus' scandalous indiscriminate association, even with outcasts and sinners? Why did Jesus not refuse Judas at least the dipping of the bread? Instead he said: Drink this, all of you.

Perhaps we cannot plan precisely under what circumstances open communion should be encouraged. But we can offer or accept spontaneous hospitality if we recognize, in the moment, our freedom to participate and to encourage one another to participate in the meal that celebrates our unity and our common commitment. Is it not possible that in some situations it is more sinful not to share a common loaf than to do so? Does anyone receive the eucharist worthily? asks theologian Elizabeth Templeton. "The eucharist may damn us. But for us to judge that we may eat and others not—that seems to me the scorning of God."[1] She continues, "If we go on 'fencing the tables,' we will make ecclesiology unintelligible to the young people of the world for generations, and theology laughable in any verbal commitment it makes to global reconciliation."[2]

THE JUSTICE OF EATING

No issue raises the question of justice more immediately than that of food. Whose food is it that we line up for, bargain over, import and export, stockpile, and waste? Is not the ownership of food a fundamental question in our present world? Or the ownership of land, of all the earth's resources, even of sunshine and rain? Is sufficient food for life and health not a moral imperative? If we take this view, we cannot separate the issue of bread from that of bread for the world. We cannot buy and eat and hoard and throw away food as if no one else had any claim or say in the matter.

Food, in all its ordinariness and concreteness, calls us to enter the mystery of our relationship with the earth, the mystery of our multifaceted human hungers, and the mystery of our inter-connectedness in the human family.

Food connects us, first of all, with primitive and sacred life patterns and processes. The gospels put us in touch with the mystery of the seed, the role of the farmer, the folly of building surplus barns. Jesus was familiar with the rhythms of the soil, with sowing and reaping, ploughing and weeding. Those who garden know something of the insidiousness of weeds that strangle growth and of the necessity of darkness and warmth for life to germinate.

I am the most amateur of gardeners, but I live with someone for whom gardening is a parable. The variety of soils, their nutrients, their dependence on a right balance of rain and sun, their potential for exhaustion; the mystery of growth itself, so close to the central mystery of all life, that it is out of death that new growth comes; the magic of a fertilizer that acts as a catalyst in releasing what is already in the soil; the exchange of pollen that makes a plant productive; the mystery of the many grains that are kneaded and merged to become one loaf, of grapes pressed together to yield the nectar of wine; the awesome abundance of trees burdened with apples, of fields flush with golden wheat, of gardens messily profuse with leeks and eggplants and tomatoes; the furrows that we plow, the waiting that ensues, the harvest we eventually glean—all these can be translated into life experiences, lifelong lessons.

I have come to savor the trite expression, "straight from the garden." I have come to pity those who never have the opportunity to pluck ripe blackberries in a country lane or rub off the soil of a crop of new potatoes. I have come to appreciate the words of Wendell Berry: "To love we must daily break the body and shed the blood of creation. When we do this knowingly, lovingly, skillfully, reverently, it is a sacrament. When we do it ignorantly, greedily, clumsily, destructively, it is a desecration."[3] And the Korean saying: "Food is heaven. Food cannot be made alone. Food is to be shared. Food is heaven."[4] And the poet's words: "Be gentle when you touch bread...there is so much beauty in bread: beauty of rain and toil, beauty of sun and soil. The winds of air caressed it. Christ often blessed it. Be gentle when you touch bread."[5]

Food connects us as well with the physical and spiritual hungers of the human family. Meal prayers are meant to express this. The gospels are filled with examples of all manner of human hunger. We are asked to enter the dynamic between those who live in luxury and those who beg at the gate, to recognize the hidden hunger for forgiveness and acceptance, to own our responsibility to give bread and not stones. Jesus was most explicit when he said: "I am the bread of life," on offer, as nourishment for all who hunger.

But hunger is not that which we associate with dinner being late, or with our periodic attempts to diet. Hunger is a gnawing pain, felt every day of their lives by thousands of the children of our world. Hunger is worry and anxiety, because it means an unremitting search for food. Hunger is grief, as mothers and fathers watch their children waste away from starvation. Hunger is humiliation, for the poor searching in our litter bins feeling the eyes of judgment upon them. Hunger is fear of the future, with its unknowns and consequent tragedies.

The hunger for food is a hunger for humanness, for security, for dignity, and for justice. The stark visibility of physical hunger in our world contrasts with the hidden hunger of those who are physically satisfied. In every human heart there is a hunger for meaning, for affirmation, for nourishment. Spiritual hunger can come masked as anxiety. Look at the faces of people on our city streets, eyes searching, brows knit in worry. Observe the young people in our high schools, hungry for life, their energies unchanneled, their ambitions frustrated. View the elderly in our nursing homes, hearts aching, faces resigned. Hunger can appear as a craving: one more drink, one more possession, one more exotic experience. What but hunger can explain the presence of a public prosecutor, a family man respected and admired in his profession, in a red light district? Hunger for the unconventional and the anonymous intimacy of sex. Hunger exists in those who yearn for freedom from domination, for a voice in their community, for opportunities to work and to live, to enjoy life.

Is hunger more acute in our world because of the pace at which we live? We have placed such strain on our relationships and our capacity to care. The boundaries of our lives are so wide and our spiritual enlargement so slow. We have not energy to learn names or languages or needs, to solve the problems of distribution. We have not enough inner security to share more generously the gifts of our earth or to allow our lives to become vulnerable. We continue to cut ourselves off from nature and its rhythms and we feel lost and deprived. People hunger for a faith broad and deep enough to sustain their finest longings. People hunger for a deeper understanding of God's word. People seek the nourishment of more regular prayer and reflection, of more stimulating study and discourse, of community life.

Our hungers could unite us to question the false gods of national security, of consumerism, of greed, of ruthless power. Our hungers could transform our consciousness, lead us to lifestyles that are more in solidarity with the desperately needy of our world. Our hungers could be converted into reverence for bread and compassion for those who are physically hungry.

Each time we gather for a meal we have the opportunity to link ourselves with those whose plates are empty. At that moment we are especially in touch with the bounty of creation, human ingenuity, and the hunger of our brothers and sisters. Meal prayers need not be a mere formality. They can recommit us. "To those who have hunger, give bread. To us who have bread, give a hunger for justice."[6]

Food is more than food. However simple or meager, it has elements of mystery and miracle. The mystics know this connection. "There is no such thing as my bread. All bread is ours and is given to me, to others through me and to me through others."[7] Some communities around the globe have kept this truth alive. The Irish who have undergone their own famines, those who lived during the Depression, those who coped with war-rationing retain a reverence for simple staples and for rare tasty luxuries. In Celtic circles not only is food blessed, but the herds and cattle, the fields and ocean, the fire and the kindling. In some places religious festivals focus on the various seasons and the planting and harvesting of food. Native Americans have always asked forgiveness of the buffalo's or bear's spirit before they killed it. Our American Thanksgiving was meant to remind us of the blessings of creation and the interdependence of all of us.

But the people of Africa, Asia, Central and South America are most competent to teach us the mystery and value of food—if we will hear them. It is they who could convert us, help us regain a sense of food's sacredness, and its power to form and transform community.

In the West, we tend to greet our friends and acquaintances with banal conversations about the weather or one's general well-being. In Asia, the greeting is likely to be a single question: Have you eaten? Their concern for one another is expressed through the medium of food.

In Africa, my friends tell me, meals are often eaten in silence. Eating is a holy act, and not to be taken for granted. Their reverence for the miracle before them can best be shown by silence.

It is customary in these cultures to enlarge the table setting to match the quantity of food available. If times are good and there are enough vegetables or corn, sometimes meat, they are shared with friends and neighbors, not put in safekeeping for tomorrow's meal.

Agriculture is still the main source of income in these regions of the world. Entire families participate in the care of the crops. The farmers are largely women, often cultivating postage-stamp size parcels of land. Children take responsibility for grazing the small herds of cattle or goats. Making meals is a ritual, from collecting firewood to polishing the empty pots. Water is often carried by hand and therefore used thoughtfully. Gifts are frequently in the form of food. Possessing little, they learn early the values of sharing, of saving, of celebration.

It is from these neighbors that we learn how unjust structures and oppressive economic policies make starvation inevitable for some. It is from them that we learn that our consumerism and gluttony are responsible for the ill health and malnutrition of their children. It is from them that we learn that food security is a precondition for economic and political stability.

Food connects us to people to whom we are indebted and for whom we are responsible. Who sets the wages of the coffee-bean growers and the fruit-pickers? Who creates the conditions that necessitate child labor and that result in the poverty of those who produce food for export? Whose land is consumed by cattle-raising so that others can consume roasts and steaks? What percentage of cotton and sugar sales are controlled by transnational corporations? How conscious are we of our privilege to choose and the effects of our choices: the level of material wealth we will acquire, the places where we will shop, the boycotts we will support, the diet we will follow?

Our food is not separate from the food in short supply in so many places. We pray the "Our Father" without flinching at the phrase, "Give us this day our daily bread." "If the bread is to be ours," says Leonardo Boff, "then we must work to transform the systems that take bread from the mouths of our hungry brothers and sisters."[8] We must ensure that the patriarchs and oligarchs, the generals and imperialists who obstruct land reform are removed.

The eucharist is a solemn judgment on our separating our affluence from the needs of the poor and oppressed. Our valid reception of the bread of life is contingent on our willingness to give bread to those in need. The community we claim within our churches is a sign of the community we are building outside, in our neighborhoods and in our world.

IN THE BREAKING OF THE BREAD

Perhaps our faith is too sophisticated, too privatized, to fully accept a God who chooses to remain with us in the form of bread, bread broken and shared. Perhaps we secretly object to the ordinariness and simplicity of this manner of God's presence. I have often thought of the incongruity of a God who appears as bread being locked up in a cold tabernacle, removed from our touch. I have often wondered whether Jesus would recognize some of our liturgies as attempts to "remember" his own sacred meal and sacred vows.

We can be sure that the bread that Jesus broke with his disciples at that last supper was the unleavened bread of their daily lives. Jesus shared a cup of wine because it was the custom and because a common cup had significance in their culture and tradition. Moreover, Jesus had his disciples prepare the room for the occasion.

Communal meals were a regular part of the worship gatherings of the various early Christian communities. It is quite widely assumed that the worship activities of the group took place at the table. Special emphasis was put on the power of a meal to break down boundaries (between classes, ethnic groups), and to create the kind of community solidarity that characterized what the church was to be.

So many of our church services are devoid of relevance and of meaningful symbols. We have so succeeded in disconnecting liturgy from life. Even our eucharists become routine stagings, mechanical recitations. We have removed from the eucharist so many human associations and human interactions that we associate with common meals. The bread is still most commonly a wafer, unlike any bread we eat daily. We sip wine from a golden chalice unlike any vessel we use in our own homes. We give so little attention to the preparation of the room and the table. Those who prepare and serve the meal are normally male. At home it is primarily women who are in charge of food and the table.

What will help us to regain the sense of a sacred meal, continuous with and giving meaning to all moments of bread-breaking? To enlarge our sense of sacrament to embrace all the gifts of the earth? Food is sacred, whether we eat at our own breakfast tables, in the company of strangers, from a knapsack, or at the hands of a gourmet cook. If we were more consistent in our appraisal and appreciation of food, might we not be more inclined to set our eucharists in a more humane context? Engage those present in the arranging and setting of the table? Gather around when it is possible? Might we not see more clearly the connection between women at the altar and women in their ordinary capacity as the preparers and servers of food?

Is it not our own real lives that we are asking God to transform? Our own real bread? Is not the bread a sign of Christ's willingness to be nourishment and strength for us and for the world? Is not our participation a sign of our willingness to be transformed, as a community, for the transformation of the world? Is not the eucharist the moment when all distinctions are erased between the holy and the common, the sacred and the secular, our human lives and journeys and our movement into God's beloved community?

The disciples' eyes were opened that early morning at the lake of Tiberias. The disciples' eyes were opened at that evening meal in Emmaus. What do we see when we break bread, when we serve one another the gifts of our table?

Our Worshipped and Adored One,
A short order cook...
How you turn the tables!
Or rather, set the table.
Do you know what you have done?
Rather,
Do we know what we have done?
Did we miss something?
(the boat, the mark, and the meal as well)[9]

WHATEVER YOU DO,
DO FOR THE GLORY OF GOD

"Then, whether you eat or drink, or whatever you do, do it for the glory of God...I do not seek my own interest, but the interest of the many" (1 Corinthians 10: 31,33).

At Hanta Yo House the lines between work, leisure, visiting, study, play, and prayer are blurred. We try to establish a rhythm of concentration and solitude, time with guests and groups, physical activity, and time for study and creative output. But there are no clear times for work to begin or recreation to end, no fixed days off, no radical distinction between the roles we play. Natural gifts determine some limits. One of us types better or has a facility with library details. Another keeps the accounts and deals with repairs. It works for us, this rhythm, this non-system of regulating work and leisure. And it works for two reasons: We are a community, each contributing, trusting one another, eliciting each one's strengths. And we have a philosophy that seeks to integrate life, not to separate it into compartments. One can relax while gardening or while reading. Professional and recreational reading often overlap. Times of silence and prayer are restful. Preparing supper takes effort as well as preparing a retreat.

Above all, we try to keep our eyes set on the larger, overall reason we are here: to clear the clutter of denominational and cultural baggage, to make connections, to bridge the chasm that has evolved between faith and life. If what we are dong is *God's* work and not just our own, we believe it is as wide and as deep as is the work of creation. It is all-inclusive: healing and making new, taking apart and unlearning, converting and protesting, celebrating and discovering.

REDEFINING OUR WORK

God's work is so much bigger than our work. If we really realize that, we are stretched and expanded not only to the utmost of our capabilities, but into a perspective that frees us and renews us *as* we work. My work may be writing a book or offering hospitality or leading a day's discussion. God's work is so much less identifiable. God may be converting, making whole and human, enlightening, opening new avenues of hope and confidence, renewing a broken spirit.

No matter what our particular job or talent may be, our work is but a tiny facet of a much larger enterprise. The farmer, the factory worker, the doctor, the scientist are parts of a whole. A mother caring for her children relies on the services of grocer and policeman and bus driver and park employee to assist her. A member of parliament relies on the newsmakers, the research staff, the secretary, the voter. In our contemporary world it is impossible to do a job as if all depended on us. It is impossible to work alone. World events are evidence: disaster assistance, international trade, cooperation in farming, technology, medicine. A breakthrough in cancer research helps persons in vastly diverse areas of the world. There are "pools" even for such vital resources as liver and heart donors. Transportation and communication systems have enabled commerce and education to crisscross the entire globe.

But we forget and even deny this network of cooperation. We have been taught to compete and to claim recognition and credit for our part in the work force. We live in a world that honors and rewards hard work, or perhaps work that "stands out." We are all driven to some extent by a success motive. Those who don't or can't work are maligned and treated as misfits. They are the dropouts in a society that runs on efficiency and competition. Redundancy is a word we shun. Retirement is poignant, marking the end of "usefulness" and the beginning of "volunteer" status and the occupation of "puttering." Hobbies are never work. In other words, work is salaried work. Most ironically, the housewife, the mother, is not a "worker." We are trying to correct that attitude, but it sticks fast.

What kind of changes will it take, in us and in our environment, before we see work in a new light, as the contribution each person makes, whatever it may be, to the sustenance and improvement of life around us? Values are in question here. We cling to long-held theories: work to be work must be difficult, what constitutes work and its value are determined by others, there is a natural hierarchy in the world of work.

In my life, I have been breaking the rules for a long time—and asking questions. Why must we introduce ourselves with a job title? Why must work fit into a nine-to-five mold? Why must I work even when my work is finished? Why is work associated with *pay* rather than *results* (not products, but results; they are different). For one short period of my life, about a year, I worked as a proofreader for a publications company. I enjoyed every aspect of proofreading, so maybe it shouldn't have properly been called work. But I was paid sufficiently for my 20 to 25 hours per week to live responsibly. One reason I did it was to be free to use the rest of my time for my *real* work, which was writing and praying and counseling.

Our western culture tends to view work very narrowly. Our profession, our job, labels us long before our character and our commitment have a chance to reveal themselves. We tend to glorify certain aspects of work. The person who has his or her own office, phone, and secretary *really* works. The space we have to work in is a sign of the importance of our work. The persons whose work involves travel, especially international travel, or lunch appointments, or special contingency budgets are a cut above the average. Many of us, openly or subtly, honor the workaholic. We often choose such to be our leaders. Even worse, we feel we must *be* one in order to prove our worth.

Who has determined the relative value of certain occupations? What deeper value system does that arrangement depend on? Why isn't access to work a human right, to be guaranteed and defended within the Bill of Rights? Would it not be logical that those who work with the frailest and most needy of our society be paid the most: child-workers, health-workers, prison rehabilitation-workers, etc.? Why do our youth rarely find their heroes in those who perform the greatest services for society, such as the peace-makers, the environmentalists, the protectors of the weak, but among those who earn the most: pop stars, athletes, politicians, TV personalities?

For so many people work means drudgery. Work demeans us and becomes another commodity that we buy and sell when it alienates us from our true selves and from our deepest instincts and yearnings, when it is not stimulating and creative. The most obvious example of this is the prostitute. But prostitution has its subtle expressions as well: lethal weapons manufacturers, factory-farm managers, questionable banking and commercial enterprises. So often people's work repays *others*, the owners of the oil rig, the company that runs the banana or tea plantation, the corporate executive of the auto industry. Those who do the labor are caught in the cycle of producing for the profit of the proprietor. To be honorable, work must offer the worker pride in the results, a share in the policies and decisions, and a just remuneration for skill and effort.

Church workers and church institutions are far from immune from these pitfalls and dilemmas. We, too, have multiplied our hierarchies and spotlighted the eccentric or the compliant. Clerics and monks work their way up the system just as their secular counterparts do. We accept that bishops live in more luxurious surroundings; we confuse servant-leadership with special privileges. We reward those who bear the pressures of leadership with extra material comforts, not necessarily with additional emotional support. The prelate who stays at the YMCA during episcopal conferences is an exception. The pastor or religious educator who drives a second-hand car is an exception. Many laity envy the housing and vacation arrangements they so dutifully make possible for the one who "ministers" to them.

Who are the workers in our parishes and church congregations? We know the roles women have traditionally played, from church cleaner to coffee-maker to child-minder to flower-arranger. We know that those who educate our children and comprise the choir and do fund-raising are working. Most of them have other full-time demanding work, upon which their families depend. Things are changing, some for the better. Women are more active on parish councils and in leading retreats. Ministers are more conscious of being team members. Lay men and women are making more decisions about worship, missionary activity, and the clergy's accountability. But we have a long way to go. Some pastors still see computers as their task rather than being companions in the community. Even women who are ordained have to struggle with "club rules." Laity all too often are not receiving value for investment.

> Then there came the ministers, following the carpenter
> but different now, domesticated and satisfied...
> And the pilgrims turned consumers
> blindly followed the white-collar workers
> into the ditch of cozy, comfy, warm
> and once a week niceties...
> The ministers ruled out narrow gates
> and substituted two-car garages
> And the only prophet they heeded
> was a journal
> from a street named Wall...[1]

WHAT ARE WE REALLY DOING?

Is it not time to take a new look at our work world and our work lives and turn some of the tables (and pyramids) upside down? To turn back to the gospels and see what Jesus meant when he said: I came not to do my own work, but the work of the One who sent me? And when his work was finished, what was it that he surrendered into the hands of his Father? His life's work, his life, his singlehearted commitment to proclaim the reign of God in season and out of season, by word and deed. The fruitfulness of his labor, impossible to judge by human standards, but fragments of hope and healing that had changed the lives of those who listened and understood.

Jesus' guidance to us regarding work can be summed up in two gospel statements. The first: "Set your heart first on God's reign and God's justice" (Matthew 6:33). Our first and primary task is to scout the territory given us and to usher in the era of God's justice. Not to ignore or neglect the needs of those close to us or our own needs, but to keep the underlying direction and motivation of our needs clear. Not to confuse riches and success with the God-given call to signal something new, something yet hidden, something very radical. Not to be bound by the framework of job description and contract, even while dealing fairly with employers and expecting justice for oneself.

We need to take time to set priorities, to discern, to reflect. This is difficult for full-time ministers, for busy family members. Taking "time out" from urgent and necessary tasks is to take time away from other people, children, friends. Yet they will benefit from our periods of solitude and retreat.

Parishes and congregations are learning that they cannot be effective in mission without times of evaluation and inspiration. Certainly churches working together ecumenically need "neutral spaces" to learn each other's traditions and priorities, to grow in a common self-understanding.

Each day's tasks are worth doing well. We are to enjoy our labor, to recognize that the meals we prepare, the letters we write, the hospitality we offer to strangers, the time spent with a hurt friend are all part of our work. Our vocation is to renew the whole creation. Nothing is left out, no effort or labor is too insignificant in the renewal scheme entrusted to human hands and hearts. "I want to lose nothing of what God has given me" (John 6:39). "Whoever comes to me, I shall not turn away" (John 6:37).

Carrying out God's work is not something peripheral to life. It is to be our food and sustenance. "Sell everything you have to buy the field with the treasure in it" (Matthew 13:44). God's work is not merely fulfilling a Sunday obligation, or obeying the commandments, or raising our children in the tradition of our grandparents. God's work is that which exhausts our energies from the moment we wake, throughout the week, all the years of our lives: caring, sharing, preserving, offering, reconciling, suffering, beholding, and blessing.

The second gospel statement is: "I sent you to go and bear much fruit, fruit that will last" (John 15:16). The fields are white unto harvest. The season for figs has come. By your fruits you will be known. No other insignia will suffice. God expects fruit. Elegant plans and carefully-worded prayers, titles and shoulder-rubbing with the famous, will be of no avail. It is futile to call "Lord, Lord" unless we are willing to put our hand to the plough, our net into the deep, our feet on the path of self-giving and costly discipleship.

God is at work in our world, in the most unlikely and unusual places. God is not limited by boundaries of Christianity, of orthodox philosophies, of claimed missionary territory. The psalms are one reference for the magnitude and the intricacy of God's creative and sustaining labor. Sometimes we trace the path of God's influence in the words of a politician, in the disclosure of a scientist, in the beauty of Indian crafts, in the reverence of a farmer or a midwife.

We cannot always measure the fruit of our work. Who is successful and who fails? Who makes an impact? Which results are lasting? Often our task is to plant seeds, to tend the seedlings. Whether we will have a garden this year or whether we are sowing perennials is not always clear. What is clear is that we need staying power, the cooperation of one another, and hope.

God is in labor that the world be born anew, in each age, in each geographical place, through the cooperation of each human community. Jesus' human life was given to the healing and redeeming of the broken and the lost. That work in turn has been entrusted to us, to transform our surroundings, reconcile what is alienated, bind up wounds, bring life out of situations of darkness and despair. "Wherever justice is sought for and prevails; wherever healing takes place and is passed on; wherever compassion prevails, the Cosmic Christ is healing, redeeming, liberating on a cosmic scale."[2] It is the Holy Spirit who opens our eyes, makes us aware, announces to us the what and how of mission. "The Holy Spirit is the invisible third party who stands between me and the other, making us mutually aware...The Holy Spirit opens my eyes to the point of need, or the heartbreaking brutality and the equally heartbreaking beauty of the world. The Holy Spirit is the giver of that vision without which the people perish."[3]

And when we come to the end of our life's work, what is it that we will commit to God? God has been at work in us, too, in our history, our unfolding personality, our relationships, and in all our blessings and afflictions. Very recently a friend died of cancer. She was a minister in the United Reformed Church and a theological instructor. Her bright spirit flashed bits of the mystery of human being-ness. She was an intense person, dedicated to congregation, students, family, to the point of self-neglect. She found so much to do, to learn, to share. We often remarked in those last months of her life how determined she was, racing, it seemed, to use up all the time that was available to her. She was forty-odd years old when she died. Her life's work was well done.

William Stringfellow speaks of vocation in the following terms: "Vocation pertains to the whole of life, including work of course, but embracing every other use of time, every other engagement of body or mind, every other circumstance in life…Vocation has to do with recognizing life as a gift and honoring the gift in the living…In the gospel, vocation means being a human being now and thus each and every decision, whether it seems great or small, becomes and is a vocational event."[4] We don't reflect often enough on that understanding of our life's work. We get so caught up in our roles, our pressures, our ambitions, that we lose sight of what it is we are really doing. What is at the bottom, what is the meaning, of our long days, our crowded calendars, our multiple appointments, our files and our faxes? Is not what really matters the depth and breadth of our growth, mutuality in giving and receiving, knowing and being known, the common project of our search for justice and freedom? In fact, we know we are working well when we are free from preoccupation with ourselves, our gain, our image.

There is no point at which our work of becoming more fully human is completed. We are in formation, in training, all of our lives. Perhaps the most important work we are given is that of reaping the lessons of our experience, our failures, our frustrated attempts, our less-than-perfect relationships, our losses. "And we are put on earth a little space, that we may learn to bear the beams of love."[5] If we are honest, must we not admit that some of our frenzied activity, our workaholism, our exhaustion are cover-ups and distractions for the work we are neglecting, the hard labor of gaining self-knowledge, of faithful availability and presence, of discerning the direction and the task that is our unique contribution to God's mission?

God works in and through us to the extent that we are open, unblocked, vulnerable. It is why undergoing suffering is so vital a dimension of each person's vocation. Wounds and heartbreaks carve us out, empty us of unessentials, so that the wind and flame of the Spirit can pass through us into the world we inhabit. So often we get in the way of that action: egoism, self-consciousness, illusions, defenses, stoicism. The parable of the seed and the soil is a parable of each of our lives, our receptivity to the action of God, our alkaline, thorny, rocky soils. It is hoped that life will plough us up, cut a furrow through us, manure and fertilize us, so that we are worthy vessels for the grace and gift of God.

Examine why you admire certain people in your life and see if they do not hold one trait in common, imperceptible perhaps, but, in retrospect, the trait that makes them authentic and influential: a transcendence, a simple clarity about themselves, an ability to see their way among life's choices and paths, and to follow despite the cost. I want to remember a line from the award-winning film, *Dances With Wolves*. There is one trail in life that is singularly important. It is the trail of becoming a true human being. There is but one work as well, and it is the same.

HOLY GROUND

Moses thought: "I will go and see this amazing sight. Why is the bush not burning up?" Yahweh said to him: "Do not come over. Take off your sandals because the place where you are standing is holy ground....I have seen the suffering of my people and I hear their cry" (Exodus 3:3,5,7).

It is the bringing together of two significant moments, for Moses, and for each of us embarked on a spiritual journey. We are attracted by mystery, by the awesome, the transcendent. We seek a vision of God.

Life is not hurrying
on to a receding future,
nor hankering after
an imagined past.
It is the turning
aside like Moses to the miracle
of the lit bush, to a brightness
that seemed as transitory as your youth
once, but is the eternity that awaits you.[1]

It is the moment of contemplation, of openness to the sacred. And sacred it is: Moses' burning bush, every "burning bush," our glimpses into and beyond the external, into the eternal patterns. At those moments we stand on holy ground.

But as soon as Yahweh has spoken: *I Am Who Am*, Yahweh points in the direction of the people enslaved in Egypt, suffering and humiliated. For the moment of contemplation and insight, the mystical moment, is never to be separated from the moment of response, of action, and of responsibility. Yahweh's identity was not revealed for Moses' own self-satisfaction and self-affirmation. Yahweh was calling Moses for a mission of liberation and leadership.

It was Jyoti Sahi, Indian painter and theologian, who brought that connection, in the familiar episode of the burning bush home to me. So much of Jyoti's art performs that additional reflective service, of connecting the unlikely, pointing to the meaning of the everyday.

How often I have meditated on the burning bush! It has been a symbol of the otherness of God, the complete inaccessibility of *I Am Who Am*. Jyoti's nudge leads me down a new path. Each time we encounter the being of another, we are confronted with mystery, with a truth we cannot comprehend, a reality that does not match anything we have hitherto known. There is in that meeting, however, a call, an invitation. Something will be asked of us, some new role will be given us. The gift of the encounter leads to the responsibility to respond. And in responding, we will find our lives changed, possibly in small ways, possibly even unrecognizably.

PATTERNS AND PARADOXES

So many of us go off on retreat, to a place in the country, to the seclusion of a convent or a monastery. We seek the way ahead, our particular vocation. But the answer is not there. Any retreat director worth his or her salt will tell us it is back where we came from. Clarity, yes, renewed energy, yes, but all must be worked out where we live and work. "Solitude is not withdrawal from ordinary life. It is the very ground of our being...Only when our activity proceeds out of this ground...does it really reach others in true communion."[2]

We read in John's gospel that "through him the whole world was made." But that very world did not recognize him. We see this mystery, this paradox, repeated throughout the gospels.

Nicodemus was blank when offered entry into this mystery. The disciples, who should have been alert at least to an underlying message, missed the meaning of the multiplication of the loaves and fishes. Amazement seized the people because what Jesus said and did was so unexpected, so unlike the behavior of any religious figure they knew. Over and over people missed the message, stumbled right over it, failed to discern that what they were looking for was there in their midst. Yet, the Samaritan woman sensed that Jesus possessed an undeniable truth. (Why is it that "outsiders" were more prone to see and to grasp?) John the Baptist, an "outsider" in his own milieu, understood that Jesus was more than he appeared to be: "You must increase; I must decrease."

Those who did recognize Jesus were often given a task. Sometimes it was as simple as: Do not tell anyone about this incident, or, pick up your bed, or, show yourself to the priests. Sometimes they were told to convert, to leave the dead unburied, or to return home. Sometimes Jesus overestimated the applicant—the rich young man, for example. After the Resurrection the task was clear: Go and tell the good news to others, go to all the nations, be witnesses of all you have seen and heard. There is a pattern detectable in Jesus' encounters: a glimpse of the reign of God is given, followed by a role in bringing that realm closer. At the very moment of the miracle, something is asked in return. In recognizing Jesus for who he was, people recognized themselves anew, discovered truth in their own lives.

Is it possible that this reciprocity is the pattern not only in our encounter with God, our glimpses of the transcendent, but also in encounters with strangers and our adventures into strange territories? Every *other* is a mystery, persons of other cultures, other creeds, other ways of life. Foreign lands are mysteries, as are new experiences, unfamiliar aspects of creation. Every *other* is a new face of the hidden God, a new incarnation of the Christ we seek, a new manifestation of the mystery of divine creativity. "The stranger is a bearer of truth that might not otherwise have been received."[3] Every burning bush not only opens us to new facets of ourselves and new comprehension of the breadth and depth of human experience, but imposes on us new responsibilities for ushering in the reign of God. "Once the door has been opened to the other, the different, the stranger one does not know, it has been opened to the world."[4]

Sometimes the *other* or the *strange* is quite near us, even approaching us in people we think we know well, in situations we think we can handle, or in places we have come to take for granted. We have looked at them so often that we now fail to see them. We think we are experts in reading our reality only to miss the message beneath the mask.

CHALLENGE OF THE FOREIGN

Fear of strangers is natural, perhaps because we, too, are foreigners in someone else's eyes. There is a part of us that is indecipherable even to ourselves. We fear it and so we fear all those who are different from us. Our attitude to strangers and to foreigners is indicative of our perception of ourselves. Do they represent a threat because *we* are lonely, insecure, isolated? Does their need for freedom and belonging call my own rootedness and vulnerability into question? Mature personhood does not come by way of repeating familiar paths, but by those experiences that explode our concepts and perceptions, so that we are forced to receive gifts that we might have shunned as dangerous and disruptive. John Vincent, Methodist leader, said in a talk I heard recently: If you want to change, or help someone else to change, put them in a place where it is impossible to be the same. Put yourself in a *strange* place.

I went to India for the first time at the end of 1981, the first time I had been in any foreign country. I remember standing outside the Bombay international airport almost paralyzed by the sights and sounds around me. Fear was an understatement; I was overwhelmed by the "other": language, vehicles, gestures, noises, smells, and above all, by the swarm of beggars that gathered close around me, each with wildly pleading eyes and persistent, outstretched hands. I had never met a real beggar until then. I had no patterns to fall back on, no reference points for responding. A few moments later I rode a bus to the domestic airport to change flights to go north. The areas around the airports are indescribable slums, unlike any I had ever seen in the United States. There were only cardboard and tin structures, gullies of mud and waste, and half-naked human beings as abundant as flies. I could not bear the stench. I felt I would not survive India. Some hours later in Madhya Pradesh I rode in a jeep to our convent in Raisen. It was unlike any journey I had ever had. I clutched the side of the open seat and pushed my feet to the floor boards as the driver, aggressive and fearless, honked and hollered his way through bewildering mazes of human, animal, and mechanized traffic. I don't think the horn stopped honking the entire fifty minutes of the journey. I arrived shaken, sick, and thoroughly grateful to be alive.

That was only the beginning of my encounters with the "other" that was India. There were foods I had never seen or tasted, courtesies and formalities that were incredibly complicated, buildings, such as a post office or shop, that were unrecognizable to me, plants and trees, elephants and monkeys, ox-carts, bronze-skinned and withered bodies. I moved in a world like a mirage, sounds and sights coming toward me, situations confronting me, for which I had no reliable, habitual response. I was always comforted by the smiles of children and the shy but friendly processions they spontaneously formed, following me for no reason except that I was *foreign*. Children, at least, are much the same wherever they are.

I have never been able to formulate sufficiently how strange those first days were. I actually wondered if one could possibly get back out of India once one was transported into the interior. Did what was familiar to me still exist? It was like being dropped on another planet. I did not know how to deal with servants. I was unaccustomed to taking my shoes off at every threshold. I had to learn how to sit comfortably for long periods on the floor or on a stool. I had never used a mosquito net. I had never rationed water so carefully. I found the prospect of sharing my living space with frogs and insects and lizards and possibly rats daunting. I was a child in a big new world, a hesitant outsider, a cautious learner. It took me at least two weeks to locate myself in

India, to begin to feel and to move with any kind of normality, any sense of my own person in this strange place.

I have written of India before and I cannot begin to repeat what I learned, mostly about myself, but also about the beauty and simplicity and sometimes the desperation of Indian people. They mirrored to me what hospitality and community, adaptability and human dignity mean. They gave me invaluable gifts of trust and respect, of humility and patience, of sacrifice and generosity. Through their eyes and through my privileged experiences I glimpsed a new face of God, new stories of the Incarnation, the Passion, new manifestations of the mystery of culture and history, of ancient faith and unspoiled humanity.

I know only one other experience that bears any similarity to that of India. It is a world about which I have also written previously, my contacts and friendships with the people of St. Ben's. I was led gradually into the radically other dimension of this encounter. I first worshipped at St. Ben's on a regular basis, finding a welcome that was unique and liberating. Slowly I realized that one could not just attend St. Ben's, one needed to become part of the community. The community included middle-class families, alcoholics, mentally disturbed, transvestites, former convicts, people of other creedal backgrounds, the destitute, and the dropouts. My first efforts to participate were in the areas of liturgy planning (not so threatening) and the meal. Each evening St. Ben's (and its co-sponsors) serves 400 to 500 people who rely on that meal for their daily sustenance. It is an incomparable event in my estimation. It is a family meal insofar as the circumstances allow. It is certainly a "kingdom" meal. Everyone is welcome, there are no first and last seats, servers and guests are intermingled, often indistinguishable. Respect is the trademark.

I felt awkward each time I carried my sixty cupcakes into the hall. My offering separated me from those who waited in all weather for access to food. It helped me understand why some who passed through the line refused to speak or spoke in anger. When I joined the ranks of those who welcomed guests at the door, I had new shocks. Now it was particularly necessary to converse with those who stood in line. How poverty-stricken I was!

What in my daily life and experience connected with theirs? What language did we have in common? I realized how removed I was from the elemental experiences that made up their lives: food and shelter, which they could not take for granted, protection from aggression even to the point of feigning mental illness, whatever pleasures were available: sex, a bit of alcohol, a joke, an evasion of the law, a chance to earn a few dollars. My office experience and book-learning were not helps in carrying on simple conversations as we stood shivering together. Why should they be friendly to me? I didn't need to be there and I would leave for my own creature comforts an hour or two hence. But many were friendly and forgave me my awkward and misguided attempts to relate.

Certain sermons were preached well in those weekly or biweekly encounters. Dignity may be dressed in rags. The struggle for humanity may shine through anti-social behavior and mental instability. Fragments of hope dwell behind bloodshot eyes and broken lives. The gift of friendship, however tentative and limited, is worth the pain of waiting. And I learned another painful lesson. When we invite the "other" into our space or enter theirs, we make it clear that our private lives have public implications.

There are experiences of the *other* that constitute a very different sort of challenge. I think of my religious community's interaction and struggles with the Roman Curia. I think of numerous efforts to "meet" government officials for dialogue about questionable policy, or authority figures for dialogue about institutions that were stunting rather than promoting life and freedom, the attempts of women to "meet" men on an equal basis, or of youth their senior colleagues. The *strange* and the *other* have many guises. And discernment is necessary where truth is demanded, or patience, or even open conflict.

I remember an evening's discussion with a young evangelical friend. We had shared some meaningful experiences and he felt like a brother or nephew to me. Yet our verbal encounter remained strange. I could not use the language of his faith. He felt the need to convince me that his beliefs were superior. We were so affirming of one another's human goodness and yet so divided in our religious understanding.

At an ecumenical meeting in Glasgow, we gathered at the end of the day to worship together in a liturgy of the Church of Scotland. I sat next to a newly-made friend, an official Roman Catholic representative at the meeting. I was not official; I was there in my capacity as co-director of an ecumenical center for spirituality. When the time came for Communion, I joined the procession. My friend did not. I found myself in the dubious position of breaking bread with Protestants and estranging myself from my Catholic friend, who was keeping discipline. The familiar became the other; the other became familiar.

On rare occasions I still find myself at a church meeting, the kind where theory and academic theology carry the day, where seemingly important debates rife with ecclesiastical jargon continue for hours, where subtle forms of competition intermingle with sincere pastoral and missionary concern. I feel uncomfortable, strange. I want to bring the discussion down to earth, to test its reality, to name some of the less visible agendas. It is a moment when I keenly feel the compromise and the complicity of church politics.

An experience this year brought home afresh the surprising response I can make when placed under stress. An ancient squatter law in Britain allows strangers to occupy an empty house as long as they do no violence in entering. A bungalow next door, owned by the churches and under our supervision, was in the process of being sold. We were awakened one night by neighbors who saw three young men entering the unoccupied bungalow. Even when the police arrived, there was no recourse. The squatters had rights. They had entered by removing a window latch without doing any damage.

I was in shock. The property was "ours." The new owners would soon be moving in. Now we had to obtain a court order and begin a lengthy and costly process of evicting the squatters. In the next twenty-four hours, we had several confrontations with the three intruders for whom squatting was admittedly a way of life. Words were exchanged, at one point a physical struggle ensued. The more they took possession of the house and garden and gate, the more determined we were to oust them.

Fortuitous circumstances (for us) combined to enable us to physically remove their belongings and regain occupancy of the house. They were not as sophisticated about their rights as we had thought. The parting was bitter and threatening. We may have won the battle, but we had failed to reach any degree of dialogue or human exchange. Our victimhood had outraged us and we acted out of that rage. It was a struggle for rights and I'm not sure that we heard the invitation that lurked behind the struggle.

NEW DISCIPLINES

The Christian vision is one of inclusiveness. The church is a community of those who converge from very different starting places. The Eucharist is a meal for strangers and outcasts who in the eating become members one of another. But only when we learn new disciplines will we recognize the *other* as friend and equal. There are no outsiders where God's generous hospitality is acknowledged.

We are all prone to shirk new challenges, simple ones like learning a new skill, or daunting ones like inviting a former prisoner to share our community life. We often keep silence or make polite utterances where challenging questions or honest confrontation are called for. We avoid exchanges that are controversial or potentially demanding. We feel paralyzed and powerless to affect situations of outright injustice. Sometimes it take courage just to name the tension in a room, to put words to one's feelings of anger or pain. It takes self-control to refrain from claiming an honor or credit one thinks one deserves. They are small moments of *crossing-over*, practice for the larger ones. We are all travelers, learning the disciplines that will facilitate the journey and make it fruitful, preparing for the final summons to an encounter with the *Other*. It is important that we know something about the peripheries that we must travel through, the folks we will meet when we arrive. They will come, we are told, from the north and the south, the east and the west, and find a place at God's banquet table. "The stranger becomes the person of promise. The stranger who comes to us may have some word of the search for God's city; when we come as a stranger to others, we may have some word for them..."[5] Crossing over is the only way.

A second discipline that will serve us is that of reading the Scriptures with new eyes. All of us have conditioned eyes and ears. We have heard the same passages about discipleship and faith and stewardship over and over, year after year. We begin to think we know what they mean. People around us have similar interpretations, they hear what we hear, so we must be right. Is one of the reasons for stagnation in some of our churches and communities that we have become monotone, so homogeneous that we echo one another? Where are the "other" voices, the diverse viewpoints and testimonies, against which we understand the Scripture message? How do we learn to see with the eyes of the underclass, the marginalized, the Samaritans, and the outcasts of our day? We are only just beginning to hear the Bible interpreted through women's experiences. Some women do not even think it is possible. This discipline presupposes that we are reading the Bible for our formation, not merely for scholarship or inspiration.

There are signs that this is changing. "The light breeze of the Spirit is a rejuvenating breeze blowing through the church and the institutions where the Bible is being studied and interpreted. This breeze is prompting more and more people to the following discovery: The real importance of the Bible is revealed not by the Bible itself, nor by the traditional criteria, but by the journey of the people trying to escape from captivity into the freedom God promises them. This changes the whole emphasis of interpretation."[6] The critical question is: Who are our evangelizers? India gave me new eyes, to take note of the mustard seed, the faces of the good shepherd, women at the well, lepers, and how they interpreted the good news. St. Ben's opened my ears to the language of hospitality and respect for the least among us and footwashing. We have all too often been looking for guidance and exegesis in the wrong places.

The most credible discipline of all is that of practicing solidarity. It is the antidote to excessive individualism, both personal and corporate. But not merely verbal solidarity. Solidarity with the other means that we both give and receive, that we recognize mutual gifts and our responsibility to exchange them. Solidarity once entered into will turn our life around. It may crucify us, for we become one with the other's pain and misfortune. Jon Sobrino says of those who embrace such solidarity: "From the poor they receive new eyes for seeing the ultimate truth of things and new energies for exploring unknown and dangerous paths."[7]

The truth the poor offer us will point up the contradictions in our own lives. We are skilled jugglers when it comes to justifying opposing values: our rights to privacy and possessions while we profess a commitment to the poor, our elaborate church buildings and comfortable lifestyles while we discuss the church of the poor, self-sufficiency while we preach hospitality. The energies we receive to explore dangerous routes will bring us into conflict with authorities and powers, and inevitably into suffering and anguish. We will be forced to acknowledge our participation in the displacement of people by our sale of weapons, by our failure to address the foreign debt crisis, by our consumerist behavior, our blindness, and our inertia. We may have to surrender or suspend our systematic theologies and our dogmatic certainties and open ourselves to the wealth of insights coming from people's theologies: feminist, liberation, black, Korean minjung...

Moses had doubts about his qualifications to be an emissary to the Egyptians. He returned again and again to argue with God, to plead his case. Eventually his reluctance cost him his entrance into the promised land. But Moses nonetheless became the leader of his people. They saw the radiance of his countenance as he spoke face to face with the *Other—I Am Who Am.*

Nicodemus, who had been afraid to seek Jesus' counsel openly, openly buried him. Peter, who had denied his association with Jesus, became the bold and courageous spokesperson for the apostles after the resurrection.

Each of us has met the *other* and missed the opportunity to enter a sacred engagement. It may have been a passing stranger, a needy friend, an opportunity to forgive or to convert. But there are burning bushes still. Today and tomorrow there will be invitations to enter the *other's* sanctuary, to stand on their holy ground, and to wait attentively. An ensuing request will surely come.

BORN OF THE SPIRIT

*"The wind blows where it pleases and you hear its sound,
but you don't know where it comes from or where it is going.
It is like that with everyone who is born of the Spirit" (John
3:8).*

Fresh winds blew in the theology classes I attended over a period
of three to four years *before* John XXIII opened the windows and
doors of the pre-Vatican II Roman Catholic church. I certainly did
not fully comprehend the significance of those lectures. I was only
vaguely aware that a current was flowing that could not be ar-
rested. I resonated with the drift of the theological commentary. I
felt the stirring of meaning. The Trinity became a community, a
network of relationships. Sacraments became sacred moments in
which I could glimpse patterns of behavior transformed and giv-
en meaning. Ethics became a human journey through experiences
weighted with consequences and demanding a careful and caring
response.

It was a new world where human events were taken seriously
and where God's Word leapt out to interpret them, where God's
action intermingled with our own. I absorbed far more than I understood. I stashed little kernels away like seeds for planting and
nurturing in future days. I was a storehouse of questions and images and ideas.

My teacher was a rare gift. Where he had acquired the scope

and the contours of his knowledge is a mystery. And most of what he talked about was mystery, not problem, a process of growth and discovery, not a static body of truth. He was pointing me somewhere, giving me a feel for the greater, grander fields that were yet to be explored. Interestingly, I don't remember any tests, any required papers. I only remember the flow of the voice, like a wind, blowing freely through the dusty rooms of my mind, already ornately furnished with systematized dogma, outlines of the spiritual life, and the moral philosophy of medieval churchmen.

I sensed the height and depth and breadth of theological discovery and I was breathless. All this interrelatedness, search for meaning, symbolic and metaphorical language were on offer. This was one professor of whom it could not be said: A curse is on you, for you have taken the key of knowledge. You yourself have not entered, and you prevented others from entering. I knew I was invited! I believe, in retrospect, that those classes were for me the beginning of an intellectual quest and the beginning of my journey into the freedom of the children of God. It gave me a thirst for probing, questioning, and making connections that not even four years of formal academic philosophy would be able to quench. It prepared me for future conflicts that would wrack my being and threaten my very sanity: law vs. freedom, letter vs. spirit, religion vs. faith, logic and reason vs. the pathways of the heart.

It was dangerous in those days to think for oneself. Better to allow others to formulate and dictate. We were forbidden to read newspapers. We made almost no decisions of our own. Friendships were suspect. We had presumably died to old identities and to any spontaneous eruptions of imagination, desire, or creative thought.

I walked for some years on that tightrope between the traditional code of clearly and neatly defined religious behavior on the one hand, and the vast expanses of dangerous and heady free expression and free thought on the other. I was appointed to chair discussions with my fellow sisters on the documents of Vatican II when they appeared. I was asked to write a position paper on the meaning of personhood for a General Chapter. I stopped going to confession. I missed my first Mass of obligation (it was August 15, 1964, the feast of the Assumption). I read widely and hungrily: *Marx and the Bible, Man's Search for Meaning, The Diary of a Country Priest, The Myth of Sisyphus.* It was indeed a case of putting new wine into old wineskins and mine did burst. It took a long time to fashion the skin that could contain the new brew.

It wasn't surprising that I found it necessary to "create" my jobs in the years that followed: a year of research and writing for the Metropolitan Lutheran Church Council, a justice and peace center to help conscientize the religious communities that formed the coalition, a national political lobby network for nuns, a begged-for sabbatical to test my writing skills and allow for a more contemplative lifestyle, resource work for the international officers of my community, an ecumenical journey that took me as consultant to the World Council of Churches in Geneva and to an ecumenical center in the United Kingdom, the authorship of four books, and more to come. I couldn't say it all in one milieu, I couldn't find the context large enough to embrace all that I wanted to engage with: local and global, church and world, politics and spirituality, community and creativity, breadth and depth.

I've been lucky since those days of classroom theology to have enough support to keep freedom of thought and movement alive and enough restraint to keep testing my vocation and commitment. I trust that this journey into freedom may continue right up to and through the door marked death, into a job I won't have to create and into the liberty that has only been foreshadowed here.

These are the linear journeys into freedom, albeit with their detours and diversions. But there are other dimensions too, inner awakenings, inner eruptions, inner crossings.

LIFE IS WHOLE

The movement into freedom is a movement away from dualisms. Is not the greatest freedom in life to be a whole human being? To be in touch with one's inner spirit, one's surroundings, one's companions, the earth with its upheavals and wonders? The churches have not all yet learned this. One-dimensional worship, irrelevant

and paternalistic sermons, stilted distinctions between contemplation and engagement are still strongly with us. Our youth sense the
distortion and feel alienated. Families search in vain and some settle for the available meager menu. Strangers peer in and withdraw
in embarrassment. The language is too specialized, the membership is too elite, the atmosphere is too formalized or too ethereal.

Our professional lives and careers often draw us into the con-
spiracy of dualism. Titles and functions define and separate us.
We draw emphatic lines between work and leisure, professional
and personal roles. I was never comfortable with the rules I was
expected to follow as a college teacher. My students were young
adults and I wanted to relate to them as friends. The situation was
further complicated because I was to be their counselor and friend
in the residence hall we shared, but their aloof professor in the
classroom.

My idea of God's reign-coming are places where roles can easily be interchanged, where protocol gives way to simple humanness, where people are unique and multi-faceted, not file-labels or
computer data. I remember meeting John Morrow at Corrymeela
as the workman who would set up our video equipment and as
an interesting lunch-time companion before I discovered he was
the leader of the community. I feel free in the company of such
people. The greatest compliment I believe we can pay another is
to say: He or she is a real human being. "Of him alone is it really
true that nothing human remained alien to him. Of this man we
say, 'This is God for us'."[1]

We are becoming more aware and more astute in looking at issues, large issues, holistically. As the Gulf War unfolded, as neutral countries, peoples, and the environment became implicated,
as prisoners and refugees increased, we were forced to look into
the history of the tensions that led to the crisis. We began to realize we, too, owed reparation for past offenses, for present lifestyles. Yet, numerous were those who saw the conflict as a clear-
cut choice: the enemy and the allies, the bad and the righteous.

What further evidence will we need before we acknowledge
that feminism and poverty are not separate issues, nor are
violence and economic recession? That economics and ecology

interpenetrate, as do military and political objectives? Until the churches to which we belong put their own proclamations into practice—solidarity with the poor, justice within institutions, mutual recognition of gifts, reconciliation of polarized factions—we will hardly speak a unified and credible message to our world. Wholeness in word and deed is a pressure and a prerogative of those who are finding freedom.

CREATION IS SACRED

The movement toward freedom is a movement toward a sacramental view of life. Children inspire us. Their dogs and their frogs are part of their community. The sand on the beach, the falling leaves, the shape of snowflakes, the magic of clouds are all wonderfully real and wonderfully mysterious. Children often possess profound wisdom. When asked by a nurse if he knew where his heart was, Pedro pointed to his two-year-old sister. After a glorious celebration of "churches together in Britain and Ireland," nine-year-old Naomi summed up the feelings of many: "I've had a good time here. Now I hope we do what we said we would." Life and meaning are concrete and immediate.

We were asked recently for suggestions for the furnishing of a new ecumenical church. What would carry the essence of tradition and also express the liveliness of the future? Tangible symbols incarnate religious and spiritual truths. The sacramental value of the ashes we associate with the onset of Lent is its power to remind us of Jewish victims and diminishing rain forests. The waters of baptism recall our vocation to resacralize the natural elements that constitute our daily existence. Candles signify the gift of self, offered and burned up, the light that cannot be extinguished, the lantern guiding our halting steps. Processions symbolize the journey of life, the experience of metanoia, the passage through death to resurrection. Anointings stretch from strengthening oil to the healing of wounds to our confirmation as disciples and ministers. Blessings extend to our daily bread, our houses, our departures and reunions, our acts of forgiveness.

We live in a world that is sacred, in a time that is kairos. Chardin may have opened this sacramental view to me. For the first time I saw a spiritual dimension in stones and grasped something of the role of suffering in the advancement and growth of humanity. The Mystical Body, the groaning of creation, the interconnectedness of reality were more than jargon. We are in this whirling, changing, diversified world as members one of another. "I will make the whole earth my altar and on it will offer you all the labors and sufferings of the world."[2] This is our morning offering; this is our worship.

"The earth is not only our source of life," writes Vincent Donovan. "It is our primary source of revelation. The earth is much more sacred than we have supposed, much holier than we have treated it."[3] The earth is not a storage closet, not a garbage dump, not a wasteland, but our largest community.

Our experiences, our life histories, are sacred. All our efforts to learn—our relationships, our accomplishments and our failures, our pains and joys—are sacred. The birth of our children, our landscapes and pilgrimage places, our fears and our visions are sacred. Nothing human is foreign to the Spirit. That is the mantra of creation-centered spirituality.

And in this attitude toward all that surrounds us, all that we need and use, all that brightens and enhances our lives, there is freedom. Who owns the rivers and the mountains? Whose gardens are our parks and our moors? To whom do the children of our world belong? For whom does the rain provide music and the sun balm? When "the world is charged with the grandeur of God" and "there lives the dearest freshness deep down things,"[4] then there is energy and motivation to reconsecrate the soil, the space we live in, the starlit skies, the seas' deep coffers.

VOICES OF FREEDOM

The movement into freedom is a prophetic one. Until the Vietnam War touched my life, prophecy was synonymous with certain books of the Bible. Liz McAllister had been a nun like me. She was also a prophet who was imprisoned for her beliefs and her bold actions. George McGovern was a politician. His prophecy lost him the presidential election. Bishop Raymond Hunthausen's prophetic words brought down Rome's reprimand. I heard these voices and many others and understood better the meaning of inner freedom. "We could not not do this," said Daniel Berrigan to his jurors. "We were pushed to this by all of our lives...I wished I hadn't had to do it...I feel sick. I feel afraid....The push of conscience is a terrible thing. You do it. And you have a certain peace because you did it, as I do this morning."[5] Freedom is following the path that beckons regardless of controversy, opposition, rejection, punishment.

I used to observe Bonnie and Pedro Cardenas in church and think: They are prophets. An interracial marriage of thirty years, a sign and call to our segregated communities and churches. I listen to our Latin sisters at a General Assembly. They are impatient with wordy proposals, eager to ask the difficult questions. Prophets! I followed Don Timmerman to demonstrations, calling Marquette University and the Army Recruiting staff and the Milwaukee business community to task. Prophets are not accepted in their own circles. An Anglican priest-friend stepped out of the promotion-track and buried himself in the social concerns of Swindon. A lay woman theologian, mother of three, speaks to bishops with words that cannot be dismissed. She is a prophet who speaks credibly and with authority.

Theirs are voices of freedom, calling us all to cross over from our protected pedestals and pious proposals into the waters of controversy and commitment. Their vocation does not arise from any privileged knowledge of the future, but from their faith in the unqualified freedom of God. So many whom I have admired and whose message has inspired me have had their words or movements restricted, their efforts blocked at one stage or another. Theresa Kane paid a price for her bold speech to the Pope some years ago. Leonardo Boff was silenced like so many others before and after him, the Matthew Foxes, Charles Currans, Jacques Pohiers. Martin Luther King, Jr. and Oscar Romero lost their lives for speaking the truth. And there are Helen Joseph in South Africa, Maura Kiely in Ireland, Elias Chacour in Palestine. Jobs and elections go to less troublesome candidates. Recognition is denied. Threats may even be inflicted. We don't expect Rembert Weakland to be named Cardinal. Barbara Harris may not be a popular bishop. The recommendations of *Faith in the City* and *Faith in the Countryside* will not be commended by the Tories. David Sheppard did not become archbishop of Canterbury. It took many years for Jim Groppi to be hailed by the city of Milwaukee for his contributions to racial justice.

But Thomas Merton was speaking of these and others like them when he wrote: "If you once penetrate by detachment and purity of heart to the inner secret of the ground of your ordinary experience, you attain to a liberty that nobody can touch, that no political change of circumstances can do anything to."[6] The prophets are not daunted. They accept the marginalization that ensues. Some of us stand in the wings, hoping they will endure and find fresh courage. And in our hearts we know that something in us, too, is awakened—a steadfast appraisal of our own milieu, an appraisal that will require that we speak and act, perhaps to the confusion and dismay of our leaders and our colleagues. Our voices may be halting, sporadic, unspectacular, even unnoticed. But it will be one more step on the journey into a freedom that has pursued *us* (Philippians 3:12).

CLOSE TO THE VICTIMS

The movement into freedom is a movement into the reality of the victims, within earshot of their cries and longings. When we begin to heal the divisions in ourselves, we help to heal the divisions of the world about us. When we understand that we share a common earth (and who can deny that since the events of the Holocaust and Hiroshima and Desert Storm?), we begin to acknowledge our need of one another. When we heed the prophets in our societies, our churches, our communities, we, too, must begin to enflesh the meaning of the Magnificat. And all of that adds up to owning our solidarity with the world's outcasts, our kinship with both oppressed and oppressor, our family loyalty to those who struggle anywhere for freedom and for the opportunity for a fuller life.

Like Job we come to see that we must transcend our individual experience, that our situation, no matter how painful or difficult, is shared by many in our world. Our very faith in God will require that we identify with the poor and the outcast, for our God has a special love for the exploited and the disenfranchised of human history.

We often ask younger people who their friends are. Who do you hang around with? We know that intimate companions are important factors in the formation of values and in making life choices. It is right that we address ourselves with the same question: Who do we hang around with?

Jesus was criticized for the company he kept as he traveled the length of Galilee, socially and in his own close community. Jesus kept close to the victims of prejudice and unjust structures. His choice of friends helped to determine the where and the how of his final obedience. We cannot go wrong if we also stray to the periphery, hang out with those whom society scorns and stigmatizes. Not only will our freedom be tested, but our very intention in joining the community of a maligned, mistreated, crucified leader.

MOVEMENT INTO RISK

A common thread runs through these various dimensions of inner freedom. That which enlarges us, our horizons, our understanding of our world and our place in it, also deepens us. It is in belonging to a global family and a global church that our own humanity and our own faith are affirmed and strengthened, that we are challenged to share more of ourselves and to make more room for those at the edges.

Numerous movements today testify to this breadth-depth connection. The recent changes in Europe have shaken old perceptions and customary modes of thinking. We have seen a Russian leader who is not closed and callous. We have seen autocratic and military governments fall and young leaders begin to build new hopes. We have seen an impenetrable wall collapse. People danced and embraced on a spot that just a short time before marked fear and danger. People chose a playwright-prisoner as president. Old party systems died and propagated an array of fledgling movements. We all had to rethink our relationships within the European and world community.

The women's movement has influenced all but the most intransigent among us. We are learning the skills of equal partnership as we conduct life's business in society, church, and family. Our language is changing, our laws are changing, our styles of governing are changing, our images of God are changing. Women theologians are prompting us to put ecology and feminism and spirituality together so that multiple wounds can be healed. In Monica Furlong's words: "I feel we are in the process of charting a new sin. The new sin is an inability, or a refusal, to look at the implications of everything we do in a very much wider context than in the past...the new sin comes with a new virtue which is a determination to connect...It is about loving the earth with all its wonders and doing our best to help and heal its creatures."[7] And Sally McFague writes: "The three metaphors of God as parent, lover, and friend form a 'trinity' expressing God's impartial, re-uniting and reciprocal love to the world...God as parent is on the side of life as such...God as lover values life, finds the world attractive and precious...God as friend needs us as co-workers in the mutual project of extending fulfillment to all of creation."[8]

Voices within the church are speaking clearly and boldly of the necessity, not the luxury, of unity and exchange. "The fundamental ecumenical confession is that we are not self-sufficient. Our grasp on the gospel is partial. Thus we need each other, not tolerate each other, for the sake of our own faithfulness. It's a way of expressing that our diversity is essential to the pursuit of the truth about God."[9] "No religion in the world," says Vincent Donovan, "including Christianity is adequate to the issues at stake today. No religion, no ethics, no cultural form, no social or political structure, no ideology can support the future that is upon us... mere internal extensions of existing religions will not be enough for today. Their interpretation, and mutual fecundation, are now imperative...It is a matter of life and death for our world."[10]

The controversial words and actions of a Korean woman at the 1991 Assembly of the World Council of Churches in Canberra reminded all of us that people must have the chance to hear and respond to the gospel in their own language and culture. Chung Hyun Kyung created the most intense controversy of the Assembly when she invoked, in dance and flame, not only the Holy Spirit, but the spirits of her own people, of Korean and other martyrs. To the orthodox her theology was unacceptable, eclectic, even pagan. Professor Chung opened up the issue of contextual theology and it will not be easily resolved.

Laity in many parts of the world are rising to the occasion, finding their prophetic voices and their rightful roles in guiding the church. A woman spoke with great feeling at a retreat: Why can't some of us preach the sermon on Sundays? We have valid faith experiences and biblical insights to share. There is strong and vocalized objection coming from places where candidates suggested and selected by the people of God to be bishops have been bypassed and conservative bishops appointed.

Creation-centered spiritualities are asking us to reconsider our rationalist theologies and to redefine the boundaries of the sacred and the spiritual. A new spirit of freedom and awareness of the pain of our world is colluding with a yearning to come home to a new way of life and a new world order to overtake or to take over the church as we know it. The task at hand is "the refounding, not the renewing, of the church of Christ."[11]

Freedom is a movement into risk. We may well be inviting suffering or failure or the loss of what we hold dear. When our hearts are small, we resist that which will stretch and reshape them. When our vision is dim, we shirk the light even as it attracts us. As our hearts expand and our vision adjusts, we become more adept at making connections and living them. "You are a chosen race, a community of priest-rulers, a consecrated nation...For God called you from your darkness to God's own wonderful light. At one stage you were no people, but now you are God's people" (1 Peter 2: 9-10).

The same promise offered to Nicodemus is offered to us. It is indeed a new life, a new comprehension. The God of surprises is very much alive. God does not do the suffering or the converting for us. It is we who must renew creation, heal splits, hearken to the prophets, refound the church, accept bolder and more demanding tasks. The promise is there, a Spirit who will encourage, energize, and empower us.

ONE BODY IN CHRIST

"Being many, we are one body in Christ, depending on one another....Let love be sincere....With those passing by, be ready to receive them....Live in peace with one another" (Romans 12:5,9,13,18).

The twelfth chapter of Romans seems to me to offer a "rule of life" for every community of any description. It pinpoints the qualities that community life depends and thrives on: humility, honesty, responsibility, generosity, forgiveness, cheerfulness. It emphasizes the outward nature of community, its raison d'être, the service of others. It even recommends a spirituality that would commend itself to the most modern and renewed communities of today, built on discernment, interdependence, encouragement of personal gifts, solidarity with the poor, nonviolence in the face of evil. It would be a worthwhile exercise to measure our own communities against the standards by which Paul challenged the Romans.

Having said that, I would like to pack this chapter away and move on to another. I have read too many chapters about community life and know only too well that community is easy to describe and tortuous to live. If we are really honest about the effort it takes to make community work, we might discourage even more people from taking it up. In my context, I see more and more people attempting community and for very diverse reasons.

New communities are also appearing on the continent of Europe, in North America, in Australia. The base community movement, which I feel is one of the most important and creative models of Christian life and mission today, is finding counterparts in many countries of the world. The trend can be viewed as a movement away from individualism and toward exchange. It can mean that the personal and the political are interrelated and that we are at last understanding the importance of solidarity and a corporate voice if we are to influence any of the powers in our world.

Certainly I believe that this trend is to be celebrated and affirmed. Community simply makes sense, in terms of resources in a world where they are dwindling, in terms of mutual support in the face of faceless systems, in terms of effectiveness of mission. Our efforts to build a world community based on mutual trust and vulnerability are futile if we are not committed to community-building at all levels. Human beings by nature need one another in order to discover the limits and the grandeur of their own personhood.

And yet so many people do not believe in community. More people are living alone in our western countries than ever before. The divorce rate steadily rises. One need only observe traffic on a normally busy highway to be reminded of the prevalence of individual lifestyles. Individualism in our western world still flourishes and is often sanctioned by government policy. We read daily of the plight of the elderly, the isolated, and the lonely.

I hesitate to write about community because the temptation is to glorify it, whereas it is in truth a checkered reality, fraught with struggle and unanswered questions. On the other hand, since openness is the continuous theme of these chapters, there would be a noticeable gap if community were not included, for it is part and parcel of all our lives at some level and in some circumstances. Community is a journey into openness *sine qua non*. It is a little like standing at the edge of a pool. One can put a toe or a foot into *doubt* or *loneliness* or even *freedom*, but when it comes to community, nothing less than a plunge will do. One is *in* or *out*. There are no fence-positions. You can't belong up to a point. That is not to belong.

And so I take up the story, aware that it is and must be personal and aware of the ambiguity of my message. Community is a most desirable goal. Community is the witness our world desperately needs. Community is a painful venture, full of pitfalls and rugged terrain, requiring immense energy and perseverance. I think we often tend to give up just when the breakthrough might come. I know we place expectations on community that it cannot bear. Most of all, we forget that community is not primarily intended for those of us who strive to create it. It is meant to facilitate and enhance the mission given to us, individually and corporately.

So it was partly out of fright and partly out of exasperation that one of our number defiantly asked Fr. Jerry whether he had ever come across a community that was authentic by his criteria. No, he replied, at least not in the Western world. Well, where then? came the retort. In the base communities of Latin America, said Fr. Jerry. Well, why there? was the next exasperated rejoinder. Because they have no choice, said Jerry. For them community is a matter of life and death. And their commitment to one another is, therefore, for life— for good, until death. I know of no communities in the Western world of which you could say the same.[1]

THE CRITICAL QUESTIONS

I have deliberately chosen to illustrate the demands and the benefits of community with some of my own high and low moments, times when the contradictions and the joys of community living were most evident. I will avoid talking about the community of St. Ben's, which has been chief among my inspirations, because I have written about it in so many other places. And I will avoid describing situations where my version may be harsh on someone who might tell the tale differently. There is no lack of material within those parameters!

Beginnings are always unique opportunities, and of course, our energy and expectation levels are soaring. In the early 1970s half a dozen nuns and priests in Milwaukee conceived the dream of a Justice and Peace Center. The housing marches and the race riots of the previous years were an impetus, as was, even more so, the Vietnam War with all its political and economic repercussions. The threat of nuclear war, the inadequacies of the welfare, health, and prison systems, a growing sense that the American people were being deceived on many fronts—all of these were part of the background.

Over the next year we won the support and commitment of our individual religious communities. We rented a one-story deserted office building just off the railroad tracks on the edge of the inner city. We furnished it with cast-offs and decorated it ourselves. We went to work. Some of us gave retreats to parish groups or members of our own congregations. Some of us monitored legislation and produced a newsletter. Some of us worked with educators and consciousness-raising groups. We began forming alliances with related issue groups, expanded into ecumenical networks, became the headquarters for various local projects. It was an exciting, creative endeavor. In the process we were a community, caring, celebrating, worshiping, and growing. Friends I made then are still part of my intimate circle. The keys to the community we shared were *open-endedness* and an *outward focus*.

But some time into our history things began to go slightly wrong. To some it seemed a hierarchy began to develop. Those at the top were exempt from the donkey duties like licking stamps and washing coffee mugs. Some of the staff became servants to those in more elevated positions. Clashes ensued between women and men, secretaries and directors of programs. The latter had privileges in relation to office hours, exemptions from accountability. The former didn't. In some quarters competition reared its head: the relative importance of certain programs, claims to available resources, bids for recognition and credit—all the human responses you might say that community life is inevitably prone to. We found ourselves devoting more and more time and energy to resolving our own differences, and resorting to personality tests and outside facilitation. There were even some resignations. Externally we continued to look and even to act like an amiable, peace-loving staff. But internally there were tensions, cries of injustice, and perhaps bitterness.

In those crucial times each of us concerned had to make an important decision. Were we willing to invest and risk the effort it would take to overcome our difficulties, clarify our mission and our roles, deepen our commitment to the vision we had all originally followed? Did we want to admit our limitations and become an aggregate of people sharing a building and adopting the usual business model of operating? Did we want to disband and acknowledge our failure to practice justice and peace even while we preached it? Most communities face these questions at some stage in their development. If the priorities are firmly owned, if a reasonable balance can be achieved between attention to personal needs and gifts and attention to corporate vocation, the community may survive and have lessons of trusting and trustworthiness to offer. So often the pieces fly in the face of conflict coupled with exhaustion, and re-composition is impossible to achieve.

I recently spent a week at Corrymeela, a community of reconciliation in Northern Ireland. While the members are scattered over a wide geographical area, a core group live on the Ballycastle site and host the programs there. During this particular week, 600 or more people had gathered to search common issues, to build a stronger commitment to the work of reconciliation, to celebrate friendships, and to worship in unity. Numerous things impressed me: the integration of children into the week's activities, the absence of protocol and privilege (there were no single "stars"), the spirit in which participants accepted torrential rain, meager meals, long lines, delays and interruptions, and the sensitivity to the strain and pain that was often just below the surface. I can only speculate and reflect that the community, both in Northern Ireland itself and specifically at Corrymeela, must have already paid the price for the degree of harmony that was so evident. Perhaps Corrymeela and its spirit are one example of a harvest of hope reaped from the seeds of personal sacrifice and bereavement and personal acts of forgiveness. In Joanna Macy's words, the heart that breaks is the heart that can contain the world.[2]

PEAK MOMENTS

Some of my most memorable experiences of community have occurred at specific events, amid the humdrum daily routines of shared life. Funerals have been one such event in my Franciscan family. They are so much more than a physical gathering and a time to mourn. Histories are recounted, ideals are reaffirmed, bonds are deepened. The personal contributions and gifts of the one honored are gathered as well: in symbol, in eulogy, in memories, in tears. Amid personal farewells, renewed ties with friends and classmates, specially chosen hymns and readings, no doubts are left about the gap that has opened or about the circle that tightens. A community meal crowns the event, and one senses that the journey has begun afresh, reinforced by the inspiration of a life now extinguished. All must carry on for her.

Family reunions at weddings, anniversaries, birthdays, or again, funerals, provide these occasions in the Puls clan. One part of the festivities of my twenty-fifth jubilee as a Franciscan was a family reunion. We needed a city park to contain us, as nieces and nephews came from afar and small cousins met. Absences were noted, but the whole array of participants in my life from childhood onward was celebrated. There were reconciliations that day, too. If ever I knew the strength and power of love, it was in that setting. Late that night we were still encircled and I watched the youngest among us clapping hands and swaying as guitar music guided our singing. Community is sometimes absorbed in the very atmosphere we breathe.

My wanderings among ecumenical communities have provided peak experiences at Assemblies, at retreats, at united worship services, in moments of symbolic action. In 1983 at the Vancouver Assembly of the World Council of Churches, I understood something of what it meant to belong to a world community. This was especially so in the worship tent, open to the university campus, resounding with song from Argentina or Russia or Zimbabwe. At one memorable service, around midnight, Desmond Tutu made an unexpected appearance. His words, authenticated by his own trials and his inimitable smile, molded one community with one clear yearning, that we might be one so that the world might believe.

One of our recent weekend gatherings at Hanta Yo was comprised of young seekers, aged seventeen to thirty. On Friday evening most were strangers to one another, questions were unfocused, trust was tentative. Through a steady process of simple interaction: talking, playing, praying, eating, listening, learning, we found a new identity. We had a sense of where each stood, what our common ground was, what supports were lacking, what dilemmas were looming. On Sunday afternoon we were strangers no longer as we posed for a group photo, celebrated the Deuteronomic call to choose life, and broke bread at our final meal together. We were not the same as we dispersed, now sent.

We need those peak moments to validate and to celebrate the ordinary tedious, difficult occasions that comprise our common life. We need times of remembering, or repenting, of re-committing. They rekindle our vision, refuel our zeal, perhaps even heal our mutual hurts. Without these events communities totter under the weight of their unmet expectations. They wither under the strain of expended energies, repeated mistakes, and exhausting encounters.

No relationship can sustain itself without injections of laughter, "time out" to rediscover the bonds still intact, moments in which we recognize the meaning we have for one another. Why, then, in our private circles and our ecclesial communities do we allow our songs and our stories to become stale? How do we expect to be sources of refreshment for those at our gates and in our care when our own wells are dry? Where will we find God and the spirit of gentleness and renewal if our eyes are dimmed by routine or our hearts clogged with tension? Valleys are not places of safety and cultivation without surrounding peaks of risk and exhilaration!

BASIC RULES OF COMMUNITY LIFE

Two of the most obvious observations one might make about life in community are often two of the most neglected practices: the necessity of mutual (even daily) forgiveness, and a guaranteed space and time to remain centered and available.

Forgiving and being forgiven are treasured sacraments of community life. We have yet to lift them to sacramental status. Stubbornness is as integral to personality as the need to relate. The gift of forgiveness is blurred by our prideful claims to be an already redeemed community. From the most serious infractions of justice and compassion to the most trivial episodes of misunderstanding and carelessness, family and community life offer endless opportunities to learn and practice forgiveness. Painfully and ploddingly, we learn that giving up a grudge, a legitimate complaint, for the sake of the whole does not diminish our personhood, our sense of justice. But standing back from the emotion and the hurt to see that greater good is the wrench. We stumble over the mathematics of proportion: the actual offense and our indignant response. We abstract the incident from its context: our own failures, circumstances impinging on the offender, pressures that bear upon all parties concerned. The final obstacle perhaps: accepting mutual responsibility. For that alone will cleanse the wound.

As I write this, I am staying in a community specializing in "care for the carers." It is one of the principles of this community to provide a peaceful atmosphere for its guests. Regardless of the struggles and clashes that may be taking place behind the scenes (and those are to be addressed and resolved), the members are expected to transcend them when they are actively ministering. If they can't, they are requested to remove themselves, temporarily or permanently.

We have all met the paradox of people finding peace in our presence just when our own last shreds of peace seem to have vanished. It is one dissimulation that the gospel does not forbid, because it is for the sake of those to whom we are sent. The fruits of the struggle to forgive, ourselves or others, are often enjoyed by those unaware and uninvolved in the conflict.

Too often we view a community as the sole, all-providing, nurturing place. Togetherness and interaction fill all the spaces where silence and solitude might reside. It is so easy to lose that balance. Communities become places as busy and as demanding as the work we are engaged in. We lose the knack of undergirding one another's solitude and of rediscovering our lost, neglected selves. Precisely because community life is intimate and intense, it deepens our need for personal space and time. The choir stalls and the dormitory cells of monasticism have their physical symbolism. Thomas Merton's advice remains wise, if often unheeded: Without solitude of some sort, there is and can be no maturity.[3] Too much community increases alienation, from ourselves as well as from those close around us. Solitude, as much as engagement, enables creativity and compassion.

Each of us longs to belong. But it is a mistake to limit our belonging to one context, one community. Not only can the community not sustain the burden that places on it, but no one community can sufficiently challenge us or receive our unique gifts. Ideally, we belong to a number of communities, in different ways and for different reasons. Some are a kind of home, a refuge, if you will. Others are urging us to the front lines, pushing us beyond our present capabilities. Some are more defined; some we drift in and out of as circumstances warrant. In some we can dwell. Others are intentional, dwelling places for our spirit. Different aspects of our being are strengthened and encouraged as we move freely among the communities that harbor us. Each needs the gift we offer. An authentic community also needs the silence and the solitude in which we all reclaim our sacred selves.

WHO WILL OTHERS SAY WE ARE?

Communities are often so intent on rebuilding themselves and ministering to others that they neglect the all-important question: Where are our experiences of community taking us? Are they enlarging us, expanding our horizons, nudging us into wider and deeper streams of life? Or are they restricting and hindering our growth, diminishing and damaging our humanity? Do our community bonds teach us the value of sacrifice and risk, of vulnerability? Or do they trigger in us a withdrawal from life's realities, a craving for our own achievements, our own place in the spotlight? Our families perhaps lay the foundations.

No community can completely stifle the urge to individualism. But communities that collude with that urge increase the damaging effects of individualism. This has been the story of societies that have exploited native populations, living species, our earth itself. "The preaching of the gospel in the American accent," says Vincent Donovan, "must come face to face with the fact that the creed of stark and rugged individualism running through the fiber of our society, through our business and economic and spiritual world, has nothing to do with Christianity. We should not baptize it. We should exorcize it from our midst."[4]

We are so acclimated to life in defined roles, with hierarchical and authority structures, in our churches, our civic life, even in family life. Unfortunately, the offshoots are often competition, arrogance, insensitivity, and feelings of powerlessness and victimhood. The "community" that corresponds to this culture is frequently marked by suspicion, secrecy, resignation, and alienation. How do we introduce and build into this milieu a spirit of generosity and respect, mutuality and compassion? How do we heal the hardened hearts of lonely "individuals"? This is the dilemma in our parishes, congregations, neighborhoods, government bodies.

Nothing we do is for ourselves alone or affects only us. The most private of acts have their consequences. How do we broaden the concept of a common life to include the very legal, educational, economic, and political systems that seem to separate and alienate persons from one another? How do we broaden the concept of a common life to include other parts of the world? It should come as no surprise to us that national and international communities have difficulty finding their way. For they are but larger versions of the communities you and I comprise. They embody the same struggles and failures, the same high hopes and the same distortions.

One of the strongest affirmations I have heard of my religious community's charism came from a bishop who knew us well. Addressing one of our General Chapters, with Latins, Europeans, North Americans, and Indians assembled, he lifted up the gift we could offer our world. It was our belief and our hope that cross-cultural community was possible, that diverse languages, customs, priorities could be pooled in a community open enough and brave enough to plod and press towards that dream.

Jesus sent out the apostles two by two, to be wise as serpents and simple as doves. He knew the danger and temptations they would meet: to count their cures, to collect followers, to claim center stage. When my co-worker and I led an event for the U.S.

Presbyterians some years ago, she gave them as an explicit reason for taking us on that we might *be* a "sign of the kingdom" as well as *talk about* signs, as women, as an ecumenical team, but especially as a *team*. In many of our circles, including ecclesial, we have not yet come to value the team approach. We belong to a long line of expert-seekers, father confessors, mother superiors, and retreat masters. Without denying the gifts and charisms of all who have taught and led us, a team style helps to forestall egoism, to lighten leadership burdens, and to balance personal gifts. But a team is a miniature community, subject to the same frictions and pressures. And our team experiences begin in our homes.

I am often struck by a phrase used in bargaining procedures. The parties involved are asked to "come to the table," the negotiating table. It may be Lithuania and Moscow, the African National Congress and Chief Buthelezi, union representatives and their employers. The image is connected to one that has doubtlessly dominated each of our lives, our kitchen tables where love and justice and communication skills were learned, our Eucharistic tables where sinner and sinned against meet, where one bread is broken and shared. "Coming to the table" is an image that brings community, whether international, ecclesial, or family, down to size. We cannot ignore our common humanity once we gather around a table. Even better if the table is round!

At a round table
there are no sides
and *all* are invited
to wholeness and to food.
Roundtabling means
no preferred seating
no first and last
no better, and no corners
for "the least of these."[5]

We have a long way to go to realize community as Paul described it to the Romans, as Jesus prayed for it on the eve of his arrest. We take small steps. We forgive the rebuff, the stinging words. We guard against egoism and privatism. We honestly assess our attitudes of exclusivity. We protect the spirit of tranquility for the sake of the creative process we are all engaged in. We probe our corporate consciences lest we betray indeed what we have professed in word. And we come to the table, over and over, to bargain, if necessary, but also to discern our peacemaking and justice building, and to celebrate our unlikely membership of one another.

CHAPTER TWELVE

BLESSED ARE YOU

"Blessed are you who are poor...Blessed are you who are hungry now...Blessed are you who weep now...Blessed are you when people hate you and reject you and insult you...Rejoice in that day and leap for joy, for a great reward is kept for you within God" (Luke 6:20-23).

Jesus spent three years training his community for ministry. He gave them courses in simplicity of life, nonviolence, forgiveness and reconciliation, servant-leadership. He supervised their interactions with strangers, with the sick and needy, with one another. He told stories, provided examples, submitted them to tests. He gave them time off when fatigue and discouragement mounted. He shielded them in the face of controversy and contempt. He preceded them into danger and derision.

He had taken them at their word when they came and asked: Master, where are you staying? There was one comprehensive lesson he longed for them to learn. All his teaching and witness reinforced it: openness to God's word, to God's way. Try as they did, they remained dull of vision, hard of hearing, undiscerning, and unbelieving. Despite the intensity of their internship, they couldn't quite muster the transparency and the vulnerability that Jesus had hoped for.

We do not find the disciples as such, certainly not as a club, included in the short list of candidates for the "kingdom of God."

For whom does Jesus say God's reign is intended? Who are those who recognize the signs of that new community? Without a shadow of a doubt, they are those who are open to God's message, to life's bitterness and blessing, to the meaning of their trials and their triumphs. They are the poor, the outcasts, the suffering, the children. Blessed are those who mourn, the gentle, the merciful, the pure of heart, the peacemakers. It is you who pronounce and comprise the reign of God!

Blessed are the Welsh families struggling to make their village-community a place of security and hope for their children, in spite of job losses and crowded housing conditions. Blessed are the Lebanese mothers whose sons have died in gunfire and by car-bombs. Blessed are the Indians of Brazil whose land and way of life have been exploited by business interests. Blessed are the families of Russia and Poland, thirsting for reform and for freedom. Blessed are the young people of Belfast, history's victims, valiant in their determination to be peacemakers. They will see and possess what most of us will overlook and undervalue. Their hands and hearts are open to community and solidarity, the present moment and its grace, the strength of truth, a living faith. They have already given evidence of their willingness to suffer and to overcome, to find new life in their openness to death. It is the ability to see, to let go, and to suffer, that Jesus seems to honor as the prerequisite for entrance into God's new community.

WHAT ARE YOU LOOKING FOR?

There are occasions in the Gospels when Jesus asks a direct question, a simple straightforward query. Who is my mother and who are my brothers? Who do you say that I am? What did you go out to the desert to see? The answer is never simple. The hearer then (and now) tends to fall silent. Is there an answer? At what level is the question being asked? Are there many answers? Is there a right answer?

What are you looking for? was one such question. I can imagine Jesus asking, much as we ask little children: What will you be when you grow up? When your faith is mature and your community-commitment confirmed? We may surprise or confuse the child. Our question is meant to indicate interest. Those disciples were equally muddled. Had they really thought about what they were looking for? Their answer was an evasive question: Where are you staying? One thing we know about Jesus' disciples is that they remained confused for a long time about their reasons for following Jesus and about the object of their search.

We were asked the same question at baptism. What do you seek? What do you expect if you enter the Christian community? Where do you think you're going in this journey of faith? And we hear echoes of that question each time we reach a crossroads, review our lives, face a heavy obstacle, or approach the end of our lives. What do we yearn for? What's it all about for us? Our answers come slowly and sometimes rife with contradictions. We behave much like the child who proffers one answer today, then feels no obligation to be bound by it, nor any responsibility to take the necessary steps to realize it.

Jesus' questions were not idle. When he asked the Pharisees whose inscription was on the coin, a very clear rationale was at work. When elders of the Jews asked Jesus who gave him authority to act as he did, Jesus' reply was a further question: Was John's ministry from God or was it merely human? They were confronted with their own deviousness. When he asked Peter: Do you love me? (one can't be more direct than that!), he was offering his friend one more chance to get his priorities right.

Jesus had questions about people's ability to see and to hear, fundamental conditions for perseverance in any quest. Mark's gospel summarizes: "Are your minds closed? Have you eyes that don't see and ears that don't hear?" (Mark 8:17-18). Curing the blind and the deaf were acts of compassion, but they were also making the point that blindness and hardness of heart, if not recognized, were obstacles to mission. "If you were blind, you would not be guilty. Now that you say, we see, this is the proof of your sin" (John 9:41). It is the lesson of so many of the parables. How do we hear the word of God, how receptive are we? Do we recognize our neighbor in the one who was stripped and robbed? Do we understand and heed the prophets who are among us, or do we actually expect to hear voices from the dead? Do we see the connection between the one who is hungry or in prison and the one we think we are honoring and serving? If we cannot see our brother or sister who is suffering or in need, how can we ever see God? If we refuse the messenger, what makes us think we will welcome the one who sent the message?

They are questions that hit home, human questions, not remote or ethereal. They are spoken in our language, not a language coded and foreign. The signs and wonders are within our grasp, our human vision. So often we are blinded by expediency or convenience. As a novice, my turn to keep vigil in the chapel (holy hours, we called them) was 3 to 4 a.m. It was a difficult time, because I hardly got back to bed before the 5 a.m. rising bell rang. But I felt privileged because it was difficult. I passed the infirmary on my way back from chapel and often the nurse on duty was waiting to ask me to help her lift an elderly patient. I resented that request. The infirmary was gloomy at that hour. I was tired from my vigil. I tried to slip past without her seeing me. Late night prayers, but blind to the need at my doorstep!

Or our vision isn't inclusive enough. We see the immediate problem: polluted beaches, surplus grain, crowded housing conditions. But we don't have a clue to the causes of pollution, the possibilities of redistributing resources or reordering priorities. We hear the cries of the civilians of Baghdad, the flooded farmers of China or Bangladesh, the starving children of the Sudan, but fail to see our implication in their misery or our role in their relief. We are numb to so many catastrophes. We watch them on our TV screens and we pass them by on our motorways. We are able to tolerate the juxtaposition of advertisements for cat food and exotic perfumes with the plight of the homeless and the frightened features of the Kurds. We have become so psychically desensitized that we fail to note the connections or the contradictions. We cannot afford to feel the grief and the pain of so many. We develop a general inability to mourn. Our experiences become more and more unrelated and chaotic.

There are voices and powers that would keep us in that state, that would close our eyes and ears and emotions in the interest of the status quo and its monopolies. Our task as disciples is to disclose those connections, to make them visible, and to be critical of the contradictions; to turn despair, our own included, into compassion. The former isolates us, the latter binds us to one another.

Similarly, some in our churches would advocate a limited vision. Theological orthodoxy, careful observance of ritual, self-contained development of plans and policies, take precedence over taking and encouraging risks. We see the frustration of youth and the yearning or the disillusionment on the faces of friends, but we don't see our responsibility to build new communities of faith, to topple structures that are not life-giving, to create our own appropriate rituals and liturgies. We do not hear the plea of Jesus for unity either around us or in the Scriptures. We divide ourselves even at the table of thanksgiving and communion. And we do it in the name of adherence to law and tradition. Shades of the stumbling blocks that Jesus himself encountered!

Just as we are being called to "deep ecology," whereby we see and heed the planetary consequences of our actions, so we are called to a "deep ecumenism," in which we unleash the wisdom and truth wherever they may be found. It is our task to insist that life and faith nourish and redeem us. We have domesticated our religious values, tamed the spirit that moves within our church circles, and thereby forced God to fit the pattern of our own realizations. We need visionaries to turn our tidy and tight structures into open patterns of relationship and exchange. The signs are everywhere. People of all ages are not finding religious experience within the organized religions of our time. Unless the church can find its way back into creation, back into the real world, with its human faces and diversity of expectations, it will surely die as an institution. In *The Color Purple*, Shug Avery gives us a clue to the shifts that are taking place all around us, whether or not we see them or approve. "My first step from the old white Man was trees. Then air. Then birds. Then other people. But one day when I was sitting quiet and feeling like a motherless child, which I was, it come to me: that feeling of being part of everything, not separate at all. I know that if I cut a tree, my arm would bleed and I laughed and cried, and I run all around the house."[1]

People are finding God in new places, and their lives and faith connect in ways that religion has never taught them.

What are we looking for in our churches? Where do we hear God's voice, God's call? Where do we see eternal patterns unfolding, signs of hope? From what sources are we renewed and challenged, are our imagination and yearning for freedom aroused and nourished?

We middle-class, well-educated Christians are at a disadvantage. We peer into the gospels over the shoulders of others. It is the base communities, the minjung, the youthful missionaries in our inner cities, those deeply committed to peace and the preservation of creation who are our evangelists and our prophets. I am reminded of Richard Holloway's words after he visited El Salvador and the site of the murder of the six Jesuits and the two women workers. "On several occasions in San Salvador, I told the people, especially the poor people I met, that they had re-evangelized me, for I can see and feel once again the power and beauty and danger of the Christian gospel."[2]

The gospel has fresh relevance for every age and every portion of God's people. But too many sermons and retreats are churned out of old files and dusty memories. The Scriptures are watered down so as not to make staunch supporters too uncomfortable. Polite words and the politics of power and privilege dim the stark truth of the gospel.

The poor do not rely on hermeneutics to understand God's Word. The Bible for them is existential, as real as the meaning of their own stories. "It's the same Bible," Ed de la Torre has written. "If one reads it to talk of mysteries above, we can fall asleep devoutly, especially if we are on top of the social pyramid, but if those below the pyramid read the Bible together, our eyes open to understand the mysteries below and we break out in joy and anger at the good news."[3]

Perhaps if we welcomed the insights of women, the critiques of youth, the reflections of minorities and the marginalized, we might read and pray anew the servant songs of Isaiah, the prophecies of Amos, the psalms of the exiles, the farewell words of Jesus. Perhaps if we gathered in our local places, regularly, with minds and hearts willing to be *formed*, our communities might begin to be transformed. The first Christians led the way. Christians today in Guatemala and the Philippines, in Korea and Brazil are showing us. If our communities are places where the beauty and danger of the gospel are felt, we may yet be re-evangelized.

LOSING TO FIND

Jesus raised a second set of questions, about hanging on and letting go. What does it profit you to gain the whole world and risk losing your very self? Those who save their life will lose it, but those who lose their life for my sake will find it. Is not life more important than food and the body more important than clothes? Who shall have all that you have stored in your barns when your life is claimed? If you wish to be perfect, go sell all that you possess. Whoever puts a hand to the plough and looks back is not fit for God's reign.

A minimum of baggage, open hands, a willingness to lose and to die—one wonders whether we have preached or learned this gospel at all. Having is so important in our value system. Even our convents and diocesan centers would have a tedious task dismantling their material acquisitions. Being someone is also important. Creating a following or building a niche for ourselves is second nature. We cling to our positions and our status and hidden, unrecognized posts are viewed as punishment. We are fairly convinced that whatever we have invested energy in must live on. Our institutions and our traditions and our ways of life are nigh eternal. Winning, rather than persevering in the struggle, makes our labor worthwhile. We tend to deny death until it is no longer possible.

The rich young man is not alone in his refusal of the good news. Not only the first disciples are concerned about compensation for abandoned nets and families. Radical discipleship, yes, until our religious customs come under scrutiny, or our family or friendship ties or favorite responsibilities are put in question.

No wonder we have such difficulty with the beatitudes. No wonder that Jesus lifted up the widow for her unconditional response. No wonder Jesus forbade Mary that form of ownership in the garden. The only way to sow new life is to allow the kernel to die. The only way God's word and God's grace can enter is through a hollowed out space, an empty vessel, a broken-open heart.

What is the most difficult thing that could be asked of us? I once would have said: my mental and emotional health. And that was exactly what was asked. Now I would answer: friends and family. And yet I know that some of them will be taken from me, whether or not I am ready. At this moment in time there is some threat to our project, to the base from which we explore and nurture an ecumenical spirituality. Perhaps the greatest test of our commitment to "clear the way" will come if we are forced to move or to give up our work.

We are slow to learn that nothing belongs to us, that all is gift. We spend so much effort defending our turf, our reputation, our self-image. We sometimes receive little from life's coffers, from the strangers we meet, from the wealth of creation, because our hands and hearts are closed. We clutch a small shell, oblivious to the seashore stretching before us. We content ourselves with a paltry diet of religious platitudes instead of savoring the riches of the world church. We claim an achievement and miss the opportunity to acknowledge those who assisted. We value our degrees and our titles, and fail to learn the wisdom of the simple or the scope of our own deficiencies.

All of life is a letting go, a rehearsal for the final grand performance. We die many times over, through loss and disappointment. The deprivation is startling and acute. The promise of resurrection is vague and often unconvincing. But we learn, in painful stages, that new life does issue from darkness and death. Each of us has to experience the rhythm of dying and rising in order to trust its pattern. "One day people will touch and talk perhaps easily, and loving be natural as breathing and warm as sunlight. And people will untie themselves, as string is unknotted, unfold and yawn and stretch and spread their fingers, unfurl, uncurl like seaweed returned to the sea..."[4]

Somehow our Christian communities seem to want to escape this route. How many communities, new or old, have you known who have graciously accepted death? Perhaps a few. But most of those I know are fighting for survival. Is there a lack of faith that dying does not mean all was in vain? Is there a willingness to let the new burst forth in unpredicted and unwanted places? Surely there are new charisms and new spiritualities for a new age! One day my own religious order will have to shift from a U.S. and European base to a base in India and Latin America. Will we be ready? Are we preparing now?

Do we who work ecumenically really think unity can come without each (all) of us letting go of some of our precious "belongings"? Do we really think that unity can be tidy and stage-managed? Whatever made us think that the Holy Spirit was controllable or manipulable? Can the laity ever truly be full participants in ministry until the clergy let go of some of their power? Can groups divided or broken ever be reconciled unless there is a surrender of pride and a mutual healing of memories? If Christians are slow to lead the way, can we expect national and international bodies to put their political and economic lives on the line?

Genuine missionaries, whatever the century or the continent, have lost in order to find. We have not absorbed the lessons of Charles de Foucauld, of the Ugandan martyrs, of catechists in Honduras. We have not followed the footsteps of Steve Biko and Etty Hillesum, nor digested the words of Sheila Cassidy, Jean Vanier, or Vincent Donovan.

On rare occasions we witness the willing death of an institution. The British Council of Churches worked its way to its demise for the sake of a more inclusive membership. Its sacrifice will be vindicated if those for whom it made room seize the kairos and realize the deepest dreams of British pioneers of unity.

The gospels all narrate the crucifixion and death of Jesus. They all contain the warnings and predictions that suffering and rejection would come. But none of the gospels ends on that note. The promise is repeated: if the grain of wheat falls into the ground and dies, it will produce fruit. This is the basis of our Christian faith. It is the central story of your life and mine. Authentic spirituality is a celebration of the original and basic gospel in today's world. Why do we think that our privileged position, our particular corner of the earth, our standard of health or wealth, our theological or ecclesiastical treasures will be the exceptions? There is no escaping the passion.

CAN YOU DRINK THE CUP?

A final significant question that Jesus posed was laden with sadness and misgiving. Can you drink the cup that I must drink? The disciples were still under the illusion that following Christ meant opportunities for advancement and recognition. He might have posed the question differently: What are you willing to suffer and die for? Or, can you allow your world-view to be turned upside down? So that those who rule are those who serve? So that those important in the eyes of others become like little children? So that the one who has most gives most? So that most attention is given to the least among you? So that the first shall be last and the last first?

Even after the resurrection, the disciples were still locked into their misunderstanding of the nature of God's commonwealth. "How dull you are," Jesus remonstrated, as he walked with Cleopas and a friend. "Is it not written that the Christ should suffer all this and then enter his glory?" (Luke 24:26). The disciples were still in shock over the brutal death of their charismatic leader. Their conception of the meaning of power and authority and the nature of the Messiah was still narrow. How many times had Jesus warned them that they, too, would be flogged and brought to trial, persecuted and run out of town? His references to yokes and crosses, to narrow gates and needles' eyes, were for their benefit, not only for the crowds and for future generations. What else did the tales of the Pharisee and the publican and places at the wedding table mean? Peter explicitly rejected Jesus' prediction of his death. Three of the apostles slept, oblivious of the immanence of Jesus' prophecies. Peter denied his intimate association with Jesus. Others escaped at the moment of crisis. What had they understood when Jesus prayed at that memorable meal: The servant is not greater than the master?

We do not deny that the first disciples were dull of hearing and slow to understand. But what about disciples in this century? Are

today's Peters and Jameses and Johns and Marthas any more com-
prehending and courageous? It is not only the clergy who cling to
their roles and expect center stage in the church. Plenty of lay men
and women resist the turning of the tables: the leadership of
women, the creative contributions of youth, the renewal of worship and of community. Getting off our ecclesiastical thrones or
out of our parochial ruts as elders, parish councilors, music directors, religious educators will be costly. Welcoming new rituals,
deeper ecumenical sharing, participative processes is tantamount
to surrender for some. Who is this God we invoke to validate our
rigid positions and points of view? If God's church is faithful, it
will be "completely mobile, fluid, renascent, bubbling, creative,
inventive, and imaginative. It will never be perennial."[5]

What about the power vested in church institutions? Has it
been co-opted by society's standards? Do size and influence out-
weigh conviction and witness? Is the sign value of the church rec-
ognizable to the underclass, the newcomers in our communities?
Can we even find the poor in our churches, in our church leadership? The Church of England is one of the wealthiest landowners in the country. Yet, over ten million people in Britain live
in poverty. In 1990, 437,000 people were homeless. In 1991 over
two million people were unemployed.[6]

Where the church has assumed the trappings of property and
pageantry, pomp and privilege, has it lost its meaning to the unemployed and those struggling to survive? A few years ago the
church in East Germany was poor materially, though powerful in
its witness to workers and young people. It played an important
part in the gathering of strength that eventually toppled the old
heavy-handed regime. Now the church in East Germany faces a
new challenge. The temptation will be to accept the advantages
and benefits that come with a united Germany, to amass property
and to earn sizable salaries like their western counterparts. Will it
lose the very authenticity it had in a less free environment?

One group who left the World Council of Churches Assembly
in Canberra disappointed and angry were the stewards and youth
leaders. In their view, and no doubt rightly, the ecumenical institutions have failed to take them seriously and to include them

in significant ways. In their own words, "We are often deprived of freedom by our churches which render us voiceless, powerless and marginalized in the name of 'experience' and 'knowledge'... We believe that the spirit of Truth is not limited to any age, gender, or other category of person."[7] It is painful for veterans to entrust young people with the future of any institution or movement. Fought-for principles might be lost, familiar patterns might be disrupted, and intolerable change might mar the hard-won stability that has been achieved. The early Christians struggled similarly, as we discover when we read Peter addressing them in Joel's words: "Your sons and daughters will prophesy, your young people will see visions" (Acts 2:17-18).

Yes is a difficult word to articulate when the suffering or sacrifice is personal and at hand. Yet suffering is a given in our faith and an integral part of the human condition. We are surprised and upset when we receive no correspondence and when we receive too much, when we are always (or never) asked to serve on committees, when relatives visit us unexpectedly or fail to visit us often enough. Trains are too late too often, weather doesn't suit, people interrupt our concentration, traffic is tiresome and tedious. We make a meal of our suffering.

As for outright persecution, how many of us have been to jail for our convictions? Or lost jobs in the cause of truth? Or taken a reduction in salary so that those "further down the totem pole" might be paid more justly? Or risked our lives for peace and justice and the freedom of others? Where were you and I during the Gulf War when we weren't watching it on TV? What are you and I doing constructively about the plight of the homeless? How many of us have shown a more than theoretical interest in the AIDS crisis?

Maybe our mistake is that we associate suffering with acting, doing something. Maybe our error is that we are so busy and so obsessed with solving problems that we are not open to the even more scandalous truth about suffering. Is our God a waiting, suffering God? Is redemption found within the suffering rather than in being rescued from it? Is that the secret of the terminal cancer victim who is still entertaining others with her music and dancing? Of the small rural communities whose land has been consumed by agribusiness and who still stand together in their need? Of the families of "disappeared" in Argentina and elsewhere who have not lost hope? Of the minority women in Kuwait, first abused by invading soldiers, now abandoned to bear and rear their children in secret and shame? Of the hostages who did not give up despite appalling conditions, uncertainty of release, physical and mental torture? Of the parents of brain-damaged or disabled children who continue to celebrate life and love?

The cup of suffering has many shapes and a variety of contents. In our tradition, the cup has special significance. It is a communal cup, meant for sharing. Abandonment at a time of suffering is the deepest of tragedies. Each time we pass the wine of the Eucharist, we are reminded of our communal relationships and our responsibility to the whole body. We are reminded that our sharing is to continue in our picking up the burdens of the larger community.

Draining the cup of suffering is the final test of our sincerity in claiming discipleship. We can expect no right or left hand seats of honor, no prerogatives of power or monopoly on truth, no thrones, no outsiders. But we can have the privilege of holding one another, broken and bruised, in the embrace of our circle, of keeping watch with the dying or keeping vigil with the condemned, of walking alongside the exiled and the weary, of standing at the foot of the cross, not in despair or in bitterness, but open to the miracle of pending resurrection. And, finally, of waiting hopefully for our own welcome into life. Wholeness at last!

N O T E S

I N T R O D U C T I O N

1. Karl Barth, et al., *Christ and Adam: Man and Humanity in Romans 5*, (Oliver and Boyd, 1956), p. 43.145

2. Dietrich Bonhoeffer, *Letters and Papers from Prison* (London: SCM Press Ltd., 1953), pp. 123-24.

3. J.V. Taylor, *The Go-Between God* (New York: Oxford University Press, 1972), p. 19.

C H A P T E R   O N E

1. Henri Nouwen, *Reaching Out* (Garden City, N.Y.: Doubleday, 1975), p. 51.

2. Dietrich Bonhoeffer, *Letters and Papers from Prison*, p. 165.

3. Leonardo Boff, *Jesus Christ Liberator* (Maryknoll, N.Y.: Orbis Books, 1978).

4. J.V. Taylor, *The Go-Between God*, p. 7.

5. Isabel Carter Heyward, *The Redemption of God: A Theology of Mutual Relation* (Washington, D.C.: University Press of America, 1982), pp. 58-59.

6. Joan Puls, *Every Bush Is Burning* (Mystic, Conn.: Twenty-Third Publications, 1985), p. 86.

7. J.V. Taylor, *The Go-Between God*, p. 10.

8. Pax Christi USA, *Peacemaking: Day By Day* (Erie, Penn.: Benet Press), p. 147.

9. Gustavo Gutierrez, *We Drink From Our Own Wells* (London: SCM Press, 1984), p. 137.

10. Isabel Carter Heyward, *The Redemption of God*, p. 75.

11. Dorothy Soelle, *Beyond Mere Obedience* (New York: Pilgrim Press, 1982), p. 62.

12. T.S. Eliot, "Four Quartets," *Collected Poems 1909-1962* (London: Faber and Faber, 1963), p. 200.

13. H.A. Williams, *True Resurrection* (London: Mitchell Beazley, 1972), pp. 34ff.

14. Hugh Neems, Halifax, Yorkshire.

15. Donald Nicholl, "Conversion of Heart," *The Tablet*, 21 October 1989, p. 1208.

C H A P T E R   T W O

1. Frederick Buechner, *A Room Called Remember* p. 129.

2. Mary Grey, *Feminism, Redemption and the Christian Tradition* (Mystic, Conn.: Twenty-Third Publications, 1990), p. 84.

3. Paul Minear, *Eyes of Faith* (London: Lutterworth Press, 1948), p. 98.

4. From a Nicaraguan Meditation on the Lord's Prayer.

5. Paul Minear, *Eyes of Faith*, p. 48.

6. Elizabeth Templeton, lay theologian, 1990 sermon.

7. R.S. Thomas, *Laboratories of the Spirit* (London: Macmillan, 1975), p. 60.

8. Martin Luther King, Jr., sermon.

C H A P T E R   T H R E E

1. Theodor Haecker, *Journal in the Night* (London: Harvill Press, 1949).

2. *As You Like It*, Act II, Scene 7.

3. John Wren-Lewis, "Theology for the Space Age," *Prismatics*, ed. Christopher Martin (London: Hodder and Stoughton), p. 107.

4. Teilhard de Chardin, *Hymn of the Universe* (London: Collins, 1965), p. 121.

5. William Blake, *Selected Poems* (London: Oxford Univ. Press, 1951), p. 121.

6. Tewa song of the sky loom.

7. C.F. Beyers-Naudé, *Hope for Faith* (Geneva: WCC Publications, 1986), pp. 24-25.

8. Etty Hillesum, *An Interrupted Life*, quoted in *Peacemaking: Day By Day*, p. 47.

9. John Dunne, *The Church of the Poor Devil* (New York: Macmilan, 1982), pp. 99-100.

10. Jean Giono, *The Man Who Planted Trees* (London: Peter Owen Publishers, 1989).

C H A P T E R   F O U R

1. Michael Cullen.

2. Mary Bosanquet, *The Life and Death of Dietrich Bonhoeffer* (London: Hodder and Stoughton, 1968), p. 245.

3. Ibid., p. 277.

4. Ibid., p. 265.

5. Agnes Mansour, *The Inside Stories*, ed. Annie Lally Milhaven (Mystic, Conn.: Twenty-Third Publications, 1987), p. 79.

6. R.S. Thomas, *Experimenting with an Amen* (London: Papermac, 1986), p. 53.

C H A P T E R   F I V E

1. *Christian Community Bible*, 1988.

2. Chief Seattle, 1854.

3. Alice Walker, *The Color Purple* (New York: Washington Square Press, 1983), p. 167.

4. Lois Wilson, *On the Road to a New World* (Geneva: World Collaboration Committee, 1988), pp. 14-15.

5. Vincent Donovan, *The Church in the Midst of Creation* (Maryknoll, N.Y.: Orbis Books, 1989), p. 74.

6. *Guardian*, Nov. 5, 1990.

7. Robert Coles, *Spiritual Life of Children* (Boston: Houghton Mifflin, 1990).

8. *Trust*, Newsletter of SCM Press, October 1990.

9. Kahlil Gibran, *The Prophet* (London: Heinemann, 1965), p. 36.

10. J.V. Taylor, "A Secret for Sharing," *The Winchester Churchman*, April 1982.

11. M. Rienstra, "To Weavers Everywhere," published by WCC.

12. *Weep Not for Me* (Geneva: WCC Publications, 1986), p. 41.

C H A P T E R   S I X

1. John Dunne, *Reasons of the Heart* (New York: Macmillan, 1978), p. 137.

2. Chuck Lathrop, "Elmer's Glue," unpublished poem.

3. John Dunne, *Reasons of the Heart*, p. 29.

C H A P T E R   S E V E N

1. Elizabeth Templeton, "The Church's Task in Reconciliation," *Theology*, Sept./Oct. 1991, p. 330.

2. Ibid.

3. Wendell Berry, *The Gift of Good Land* (San Francisco: North Point Press, 1981), p. 281.

4. Kim Chi Ha, Korean poet, quoted in *Your Kingdom Come* (Christian Conference of Asia, 1980), p. 17.

5. Anonymous.

6. Prayer from Latin America.

7. Meister Eckhart, quoted in Matthew Fox, *Original Blessing* (Santa Fe N.M.: Bear and Company, 1983), p. 265.

8. Leonardo Boff, *The Lord's Prayer: The Prayer of Integral Liberation* (Maryknoll, N.Y.: Orbis Books, 1984).

9. Chuck Lathrop, *A Gentle Presence* (Washington, D.C.: Appalachian Documentation, 1977), p. 27.

C H A P T E R   E I G H T

1. Chuck Lathrop, "Basic Carpentry," unpublished poem.

2. Matthew Fox, *The Coming of the Cosmic Christ* (San Francisco: Harper & Row, 1988), p. 153.

3. J.V. Taylor, *The Go-Between God*, p. 19.

4. William Stringfellow, *The Politics of Spirituality* (Philadelphia: Westminster Press, 1984).

5. William Blake, *Selected Poems*, p. 41.

C H A P T E R   N I N E

1. R. S. Thomas, *Later Poems 1972-1982* (London: Macmillan, 1983), p. 81.

2. Thomas Merton, *Love and Living* (London: Sheldon Press), pp. 23-24.

3. Parker J. Palmer, *The Company of Strangers* (New York: Crossroad, 1986), p. 58.

4. Ann Loades, ed., *Feminist Theology: A Reader* (London: SPCK, 1990), p. 273.

5. Parker J. Palmer, *The Company of Strangers*, p. 64.

6. Carlos Mesters, *Defenseless Flower* (Maryknoll, N.Y.: Orbis Books, 1989), p. 24.

7. Jon Sobrino, *Theology of Christian Solidarity* (Maryknoll, N.Y.: Orbis Books, 1985), p. 11.

C H A P T E R   T E N

1. Dietrich Bonhoeffer, *Christology* (London: Collins, 1966), p. 107.

2. Teilhard de Chardin, *Hymn of the Universe* (New York: Harper Collins, 1965), p. 19.

3. Vincent Donovan, *The Church in the Midst of Creation*, p. 123.

4. Gerard Manley Hopkins, *A Selection of His Poems and Prose*, (London: Penguin Books, 1953), p. 27.

5. Quoted in *Peacemaking: Day by Day*, p. 86.

6. Thomas Merton, *Asian Journal* (New York: New Directions, 1968), pp. 316-317.

7. Monica Furlong, "Connect and Collect," *The Tablet*, 24 March 1990, p. 380.

8. Sally McFague, *Models of God* (Philadelphia: Fortress Press, 1987), pp. 91-92.

9. Michael Kinnamon, *Assembly Line* (WCC Seventh Assembly, 18 Feb. 1991), p. 8.

10. Vincent Donovan, *The Church in the Midst of Creation*, p. 143.

11. Ibid., p. 34.

C H A P T E R   E L E V E N

1. Donald Nicholl, *The Testing of Hearts* (London: Lamp Press, 1989), p. 144.

2. Anne Bancroft, *Weavers of Wisdom* (London: Arkana, 1989), p. 8.

3. Thomas Merton, *Love and Living*, p. 21.

4. Vincent Donovan, *The Church in the Midst of Creation*, p. 137.

5. Chuck Lathrop, *A Gentle Presence*, p. 7.

C H A P T E R   T W E L V E

1. Alice Walker, *The Color Purple*, p. 167.

2. Richard Holloway, Testimony, June 1990.

3. Ed de la Torre, Source unknown.

4. A.S.J. Tessimond, *Collected Poems*, ed. H. Nicholson (Whiteknights Press, 1985), p. 48.

5. Jacques Ellul, *The Subversion of Christianity*, quoted in *Resurgence*, March/April 1990, p. 49.

6. From *Church Action on Poverty*, Manchester, UK.

7. Youth Message, Canberra Assembly of WCC, Feb. 1991.

OTHER TITLES BY SR. JOAN PULS

EVERY BUSH IS BURNING
A Spirituality for Our Times

Drawing upon contemporary events, personal stories, the world of nature and the world of contemplation, Joan Puls develops an incarnational approach to spirituality along the themes of life: searching, formation, conflict, obedience, freedom and exchange. The book explores the links between personal spirituality and an ecumenical and global spirituality.

ISBN: 0-89622-280-2, 102 pages, $5.95

HEARTS SET ON THE PILGRIMAGE
The Challenge of Discipleship in a World Church

Joan Puls answers the question "What is being asked of Christian communities, of each of us as disciples, as the twentieth century becomes the twenty-first?" Her approach is practical, ecumenical and deeply spiritual, reflecting on the church as pilgrim, as servant and as hospitable community. The book honors the laity, asks hard questions of all professed Christians and offers suggestions to those who struggle to be faithful to the teachings of Christ.

ISBN: 0-89622-403-1, 117 pages, $7.95

A SPIRITUALITY OF COMPASSION

The book is an invitation to readers to live the compassion necessary to heal the wounds in personal and communal lives that result from loneliness, brokenness and despair—any situation threatening the quality of human life. Joan Puls believes that life is lived in constantly evolving experiences of exchange between individuals and among communities of people—an exchange that underlies an interdependence necessary for healing, growth and bonding.

ISBN: 0-89622-352-3, 134 pages, $7.95

Available through Spiritual Book Associates
or from **TWENTY-THIRD PUBLICATIONS**
P.O. Box 180 • Mystic, CT 06355 • 1-800-321-0411